NOMICAL HISTORY

JANUARY

Nomical History

January

by Joel Thomas

For Olivia,

Whose wit, humor, and kindness remind me daily that history's most important moments aren't always the ones that make it into books. Thank you for being such a wonderful part of my life and for proving that the future is in good hands.

PREFACE

History rarely arrives in neat, well organized series of events. More often, it stumbles forward through accidents, arguments, coincidences, and moments that only look inevitable when viewed in reverse. The Nomical History Monthly series exists to examine those moments as they happened, and to show how a single month can carry upheaval, invention, collapse, celebration, and decisions whose consequences stretch far beyond their original authors.

January may be the first page of the calendar, but it is never the quietest.

This volume follows the same method as the rest of the series, treating each date as a junction where human intent collides with unintended consequences. The aim is simple, strip events of their polished mythology and expose the machinery underneath, whether it is powered by courage, incompetence, luck, stubbornness, or some combination of all four. January's entries range from ancient turning points to modern crises, from rituals that shaped cultures to decisions that reshaped nations, each one a reminder that history is built from ordinary moments carrying extraordinary weight.

This book is not an archive of heroes and villains. It is a record of pressure, choice, and consequence. It focuses on people acting with limited information, flawed judgment, and competing priorities, pushing the world forward, backward, or sideways without knowing which direction would last.

Lastly, the irreverent tone is not the goal; it serves only as a means to challenge convention and provoke thought, rather than to disrespect or diminish the subject. The objective remains unchanged, to make the past clear enough to understand and sharp enough to feel.

CONTENTS

INTRODUCTION

January is where consequences wake up. The calendar resets, resolutions are declared, and the world pretends novelty has arrived simply because the numbering changed. History disagrees. January is not a beginning in any meaningful sense beyond the calendar itself. It is the moment when decisions made earlier start producing results, often faster than anyone planned and usually louder than expected. Systems stressed in December either stabilize or break. Movements either gain traction or collapse under their own weight. January is where momentum becomes visible for better, or worse.

This month carries a particular kind of clarity. There is no seasonal illusion of winding down. Armies still advance. Governments still assert authority. Revolutions test their durability or collapse. Ideas either survive from first contact with reality or fail outright. January has little patience for symbolism. It favors action, enforcement, and exposure. If something cannot function when the year begins, it rarely lasts long enough to see spring.

This volume treats January as proving ground. New regimes announce themselves. Treaties are tested. Explorations begin. Scientific work moves from theory into practice. Cultural shifts accelerate because hesitation has expired. The events collected here show how quickly optimism gives way to structure, and how often ambition collides with limits that were always present but temporarily ignored.

Each entry isolates a single day and examines what happened, why it mattered, and how its effects propagated outward, sometimes immediately, sometimes across centuries. The tone remains direct. The humor remains surgical. The purpose remains unchanged, to remove the comfort of hindsight and replace it with understanding.

January exposes a simple truth. Beginnings are not clean, they are often confrontational. The year does not always open with possibility. It sometimes opens with pressure. What survives January usually defines everything that follows, history is the proof of that.

CHAPTER 1

BEGINNINGS THAT REDEFINED THE WORLD

THE ARCHITECTURE OF BEGINNINGS

January is treated as the beginning of the year, but the events in this chapter show that real beginnings do not obey the calendar. They appear when existing systems reach their limits and the people inside them decide that drifting is no longer an option. A continent tired of acting like six countries becomes one. A new republic tests whether elections can hold a fractured union together. A state with more wilderness than infrastructure declares that education is worth founding before roads are finished. These moments are not dramatic; they are procedural. They look like paperwork to outsiders, but they alter the direction of nations.

What links these origins is the quiet admission that the old arrangements have failed. A treaty must be signed because victory alone does not create a country. A constitution must be written because independence without structure is a slogan, not a system. A medical breakthrough must be institutionalized because diagnosis without treatment is a slow-moving death sentence. A humanitarian network must be formalized because good intentions collapse under the weight of uncoordinated response. All of these actions share the same underlying logic: build something that can outlast the crisis that created it.

The people involved were not mythic founders. They were administrators, legislators, scientists, and ordinary citizens doing work that produces stability instead of spectacle. Their actions remind us that nations do not endure through passion or identity alone. They endure through systems able to withstand pressure, absorb conflict, and remain functional when the people who built them are gone. These events are beginnings not because they were celebrated, but because they created frameworks strong enough to carry everything that followed.

Life Lesson: Lasting change is built, not declared. If you want something to endure, give it structure, give it rules, and give it the stability that emotion cannot provide.

1/1/1901 COMMONWEALTH OF AUSTRALIA IS FORMED

A CONTINENT TIRED OF ARGUING DECIDES TO BECOME A NATION

Australia entered the new century with a simple diagnosis of its political condition, six colonies were wasting too much time acting like six countries. For decades they had maintained separate tariffs, incompatible rail systems, and a regional rivalry that made cooperation feel like an occasional accident. By 1 January 1901, the colonies concluded they could either continue bickering over whose trains should fit on whose tracks, or they could assemble something resembling a nation. Federation was the answer, not glamorous, not revolutionary, but unmistakably necessary.

The push toward unification had been building since the 1880s. Trade disputes clogged commerce. Border controls frustrated travelers. Duplicated government agencies drove costs up while patience went down. Colonial leaders held conventions through the 1890s to shape a federal constitution, arguing about representation, taxation, and how to balance the larger states against the smaller ones. It was the driest kind of politics, the sort that manages to be essential and tedious at the same time. But the delegates kept at it because the alternative was a continent arranged like a family that refused to share a kitchen.

By the decade's end, the draft constitution reached the public. Referendums across the colonies returned results that were clear enough even for cautious politicians. The people wanted federation. They were ready for a national government capable of negotiating trade, coordinating defense, and eliminating the bureaucratic chore of paying tariffs every time someone crossed an invisible line in the bush.

Britain approved the plan with a mix of amusement and relief. The Crown was happy to retain influence without overseeing the internal quarrels of six distant colonies. Queen Victoria signed the proclamation establishing the Commonwealth of Australia, and on 1 January 1901, the new nation took its first legal breath. No shots were fired. No statues toppled. The revolution came in the form of signatures, stamps, and the quiet satisfaction of a continent that had finally organized its paperwork.

The fledgling Commonwealth inherited both opportunity and contradiction. It possessed vast land, growing cities, and a population eager to define its identity. But it also carried old prejudices, most notably in the form of the White Australia Policy, which became the new government's first major legislative act. The contradiction was not unique. Nations often begin with ideals and blind spots in unequal proportion.

Even with its faults, federation gave Australia a structure capable of adaptation. The new parliament in Melbourne (later Canberra) began shaping national policy. Trade barriers between states vanished. A unified defense system emerged. The High Court clarified constitutional boundaries. Australia behaved like a country determined to grow into its responsibilities without losing its preference for informality.

Despite early dependence on Britain, true autonomy expanded steadily. Participation in global conflicts, new trade relationships, and eventual legal independence through the Statute of Westminster Adoption Act (1942) and Australia Act (1986) completed the transformation that began on that January morning. What started as administrative coordination evolved into a mature national identity.

Australia's birth was unusual for its calm. Many nations arrive through fire. This one arrived through ballots, conventions, and the collective realization that cooperation was cheaper than rivalry. It was an achievement built not on dramatic moments but on deliberate ones, the kind of careful nation building that rarely becomes legend yet defines a country far more reliably than myths.

Takeaway: Australia's federation proved that nationhood can begin without gunpowder, requiring only patience, paperwork, and the shared recognition that six governments are five too many.

1/1/1920 LEAGUE OF NATIONS FOUNDED
AN AMBITIOUS ATTEMPT AT PEACE MISSING THE ONE MEMBER WHO INVENTED IT

The League of Nations was formally established on 10 January 1920, emerging from the wreckage of World War I as humanity's first organized attempt to prevent future global conflict. Woodrow Wilson had championed the idea, believing that diplomacy could be institutionalized and war deterred through collective security. The League's covenant promised that member nations would resolve disputes peacefully and stand united against aggression. It was a bold vision, shaped by optimism and necessity.

Plenary session which adopted the first of the Covenant of the League of Nations

Reality, however, intruded immediately. The United States—the architect of the League—failed to join. The Senate rejected membership, fearing entanglement in foreign conflicts.

The absence crippled the institution before it began. Without the world's rising superpower, enforcement became theoretical. Resolutions lacked teeth. Collective security became a promise with no sheriff.

Still, the League pursued its mandate. It mediated border disputes, supervised mandates, addressed minority rights, and worked on labor standards, health initiatives, and disarmament proposals. These efforts were not failures; they were simply overshadowed by the League's inability to contain the growing aggression of the 1930s. Japan invaded Manchuria. Italy invaded Ethiopia. Germany rearmed. Each crisis revealed the League's structural weakness: it could condemn but not compel.

The organization's influence dwindled as authoritarian regimes ignored its warnings. By the time World War II erupted, the League existed more on paper than in politics. In 1946 it dissolved, transferring its assets and aspirations to the newly created United Nations.

Despite its shortcomings, the League of Nations mattered. It established the blueprint for modern internationalism and demonstrated that cooperation, however flawed, was preferable to the isolation that preceded global catastrophe. Its legacy is visible in the UN, international courts, humanitarian organizations, and the assumption that diplomacy requires architecture, not improvisation.

Takeaway: The League of Nations proved that good ideas fail without power behind them, and that peace needs more than promises to survive ambitious nations with short tempers.

1/7/1789 FIRST U.S. PRESIDENTIAL ELECTION HELD
A NEW REPUBLIC TESTS WHETHER BALLOTS CAN REPLACE BAYONETS

The United States held its first presidential election in January 1789, a political experiment so unprecedented that even the participants were not entirely sure how smoothly it would run. The Constitution had been ratified only months earlier. The federal government existed mostly on parchment and optimism. The nation's stability rested on the assumption that citizens would cast ballots without starting another revolution and that the electoral system, built on compromise and calculations, would function exactly as written rather than exactly as feared.

Only ten of the thirteen states participated; North Carolina and Rhode Island had not yet ratified the Constitution, and New York's legislature failed to choose electors in time. Still, the process proceeded. State legislatures selected electors, who in turn would vote for two candidates each. The candidate with the most electoral votes would become president, the runner up vice president. It was a system designed by men who assumed political parties were a temporary inconvenience rather than an approaching inevitability.

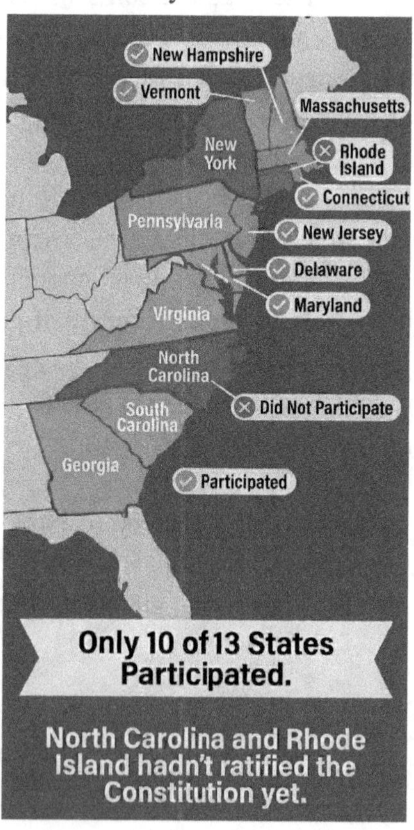

Everyone knew the outcome before the ballots were cast. George Washington was the only figure with enough stature, neutrality, and national respect to lead a country still unsure of its political identity. His reputation as a commander who had refused kingship made him the safest possible choice. Electors voted accordingly. Washington received every vote, becoming the first and last president unanimously elected. John Adams finished second, earning the vice presidency through the peculiar arithmetic the Constitution demanded.

The election revealed both the strengths and weaknesses of the new system. It demonstrated the peaceful transfer of authority, the legitimacy of constitutional procedures, and the public's willingness to support a central executive. But it also exposed underlying tensions. States varied widely in how electors were chosen. Some allowed popular input; others did not. The Electoral College's structure, intended to filter public will through deliberation, already resembled a compromise no one fully admired.

Washington accepted the result with reluctance. He preferred retirement at Mount Vernon but recognized that the republic needed a stabilizing figure to guide its fragile beginning. When he traveled to New York City for his inauguration, crowds gathered along the route, sensing that the nation had managed something rare: a peaceful election that produced a leader rather than a crisis.

The first presidential election set a precedent that future generations would interpret, challenge, and reshape. It demonstrated that the Constitution could function under real conditions rather than theoretical ones. It also revealed that Americans expected elections to legitimize leadership, not merely ratify elite decisions. Over time, the electoral system would evolve, parties would rise, and the once simple process would become a battleground for ideology, ambition, and public opinion. But in 1789, the goal was survival, and the system achieved it.

Takeaway: America's first presidential election proved that a republic can begin with ballots instead of bloodshed, and that sometimes the safest choice for a new nation is the one man everyone already trusts not to ruin it.

1/9/1799 Income Tax Introduced in Britain
The prime minister invents a temporary tax to fight Napoleon, and governments everywhere decide temporary means forever

A prime minister invents a temporary tax to fight Napoleon, and governments everywhere decide that temporary means permanent.

William Pitt the Younger introduced income tax in Britain on 9 January 1799, presenting it as an emergency measure to fund the war against Napoleon. It would be temporary, he promised—just until the crisis passed. The crisis passed. The tax remained. Governments worldwide took notes, realizing they had discovered a revenue stream far more reliable than tariffs, land taxes, or occasional church confiscations. Pitt had constructed the financial architecture that would power modern states, fund welfare systems, and ensure that April became the month when everyone remembers why they resent their government.

Britain was desperate. The war with Revolutionary France had drained the treasury. Traditional revenue sources—customs duties, excise taxes, property assessments—could not keep pace with military expenditures. Pitt needed money immediately and proposed something radical: tax people directly on their earnings rather than indirectly through goods purchased.

The idea was not entirely new, but none had implemented a systematic, graduated income tax collected annually from the entire working population. Pitt's plan divided income into brackets and taxed higher earners at higher rates—progressive taxation before economists gave it a proper name. Those earning under £60 annually paid nothing. Those above paid a sliding scale up to 10 percent on incomes exceeding £200.

Public reaction ranged from outrage to resignation. The wealthy protested government intrusion. Privacy advocates argued the state had no business knowing earnings. Pitt countered that the alternative was losing the war, and most Britons preferred taxation to French occupation. The tax passed, enforcement began, and revenue flowed.

The system worked—too well for its own advertised temporariness. When peace arrived in 1802, the income tax was repealed amid celebration. Citizens burned their tax records in public demonstrations. The celebration lasted fourteen months. War resumed in 1803, and with it came the income tax, now called "Property Tax" as if vocabulary would soften the blow. This time the tax stayed. After Napoleon's defeat in 1815, Parliament voted to abolish it again, even ordering records destroyed to prevent resurrection. The gesture was theatrical but pointless. By 1842, Prime Minister Robert Peel reintroduced income tax—again as temporary—to address budget deficits. It never left. Governments learned that emergency powers, once granted, rarely expire.

The income tax transformed the relationship between citizens and the state. Before its introduction, governments taxed transactions, property, and goods—interactions people could sometimes avoid. Income tax was inescapable. The system required new bureaucracies to assess, collect, and enforce compliance. Tax collectors became permanent fixtures. Accountants emerged as essential professionals. Evasion became a national pastime.

Other nations adopted their own versions. The United States introduced income tax during the Civil War, repealed it, then brought it back permanently with the 16th Amendment in 1913. By the mid-twentieth century, most industrialized nations had embraced progressive income taxation. What started as Pitt's wartime necessity became the standard method for funding governments worldwide.

The income tax enabled the modern welfare state. Universal healthcare, public education, social security, infrastructure—all required revenue streams that property taxes and tariffs could not sustain. It also made governments far larger than earlier generations imagined possible, proving that state size correlates directly with its ability to extract resources from the population.

Pitt died in 1806, never seeing his temporary measure become permanent or spread globally. Once governments discover an efficient way to collect revenue, they do not surrender it voluntarily. The income tax began as an innovation to save Britain from Napoleon. It ended as the mechanism that transformed nations into bureaucracies capable of monitoring earnings, enforcing compliance, and funding ambitions previous governments could not afford to pursue.

Takeaway: Pitt's income tax proved that nothing is more permanent than a temporary government program, and that once the state learns to reach directly into your paycheck, it never learns to let go.

1/11/1922 FIRST HUMAN RECEIVES INSULIN
A MEDICAL BREAKTHROUGH TRANSFORMS DIABETES FROM A DEATH SENTENCE INTO A TREATABLE CONDITION

A fourteen-year-old boy named Leonard Thompson became the first human to receive an injection of purified insulin, marking a turning point in medical history. Before insulin therapy, Type 1 diabetes was a brutal and terminal diagnosis. Patients wasted away despite starvation diets that prolonged life only briefly. The disease advanced inexorably. Physicians could diagnose diabetes, but they could not treat it. That changed in a Toronto hospital when science, persistence, and desperation converged.

Frederick Banting and Charles Best

The breakthrough stemmed from the work of Frederick Banting, Charles Best, John Macleod, and James Collip. Banting, a surgeon with an idea but no laboratory, persuaded Macleod to give him space and a student assistant. Using dogs as experimental subjects, Banting and Best isolated a substance from the pancreas that controlled blood sugar. The initial extract was crude, but promising. Collip later refined the preparation into something safe enough for human use.

Thompson received the first injection, but the extract was still imperfect. The results were disappointing. Collip intensified his efforts, producing a cleaner, more effective batch. Twelve days later, January 23rd, Thompson received a second injection. This time the improvement was immediate. His blood sugar dropped. His symptoms receded. His life, once slipping toward inevitability, was suddenly salvageable.

News of the breakthrough spread rapidly. Within months, insulin was being produced for broader clinical use. Children and adults who had been wasting away in hospital wards improved visibly, gaining weight and returning to ordinary life. It was one of the rare moments in medicine when an incurable disease met its match almost overnight.

The scientific world awarded Banting and Macleod the Nobel Prize in 1923, prompting Banting to share his portion with Best and complain that the committee had misunderstood the contributions. Disputes aside, the therapy revolutionized endocrinology and reshaped expectations of what medical science could achieve. Pharmaceutical companies began large scale production, refining formulations and enabling global distribution.

Insulin did not cure diabetes; it managed it. But management was the difference between death and life. Millions would go on to depend on the hormone daily. Modern versions, from analog insulins to pumps, trace their lineage to that January day when a boy's survival proved that disease could lose decisively.

Takeaway: The first successful insulin injection proved that medical breakthroughs often arrive through persistence and improvisation, and that a single treatment can redraw the boundary between fatal and manageable.

1/12/1804 HAITI GAINS INDEPENDENCE
ENSLAVED PEOPLE DEFEAT AN EMPIRE AND FORCE THE WORLD TO CONFRONT ITS CONTRADICTIONS

Haiti declared independence in January 1804, becoming the first Black republic and the first nation born from a successful slave revolt. The victory capped the Haitian Revolution, which began in 1791 as an uprising against French colonial rule in Saint-Domingue, then the wealthiest plantation colony on Earth. Over thirteen years of shifting alliances, scorched earth campaigns, and revolutionary improvisation, the enslaved population dismantled a racial and economic hierarchy that Europe had considered permanent.

Toussaint Louverture emerged during the revolution's early and middle phases as a brilliant strategist and political leader, navigating internal divisions while fending off invasions by France, Britain, and Spain. His attempt to stabilize the colony under nominal French authority ultimately made him dangerous to Napoleon. He was captured by deceit, shipped to France, and left to die in prison, clearing the way for a more uncompromising conclusion.

That conclusion came under Jean-Jacques Dessalines. Where Toussaint negotiated, Dessalines finished the war. He led the final campaign that destroyed the remaining French forces, shattered Napoleon's Caribbean ambitions, and formally proclaimed Haiti an independent state. France lost its most profitable colony, along with tens of thousands of soldiers and any illusions about restoring slavery there.

The revolution terrified slaveholding nations. It was not just a military defeat but a philosophical one. Haiti exposed the contradiction at the heart of empires that preached liberty while depending on bondage. European powers refused to recognize the new republic. The United States, founded on its own revolution, declined recognition as well, waiting until 1862 to acknowledge a nation that had done what it preferred its enslaved population never attempt.

Haiti endured anyway. In the years that followed, it faced diplomatic isolation, trade embargoes, and in 1825 a punitive indemnity imposed by France, which demanded compensation for the loss of enslaved people euphemistically labeled "property." The new nation inherited devastation, plantations burned, cities ruined, and an economy deliberately strangled. It responded by establishing a constitution that abolished slavery permanently and declared freedom nonnegotiable.

The revolution's consequences rippled outward. It helped convince Napoleon to abandon dreams of a New World empire and sell Louisiana, reshaping North America. It altered the calculus of colonial rule throughout the Caribbean and Latin America. It proved that emancipation could be seized rather than scheduled.

Haiti struggled afterward with political instability, foreign interference, and debt engineered to ensure it never fully recovered. None of that diminishes the achievement. An enslaved population confronted the most powerful empires of its age, defeated them on the battlefield, and forced the world to accept a truth it desperately tried to avoid.

Takeaway: Haiti's independence proved that liberation does not require approval, and that when the oppressed overturn the logic of empire, the world responds not with applause, but with fear, punishment, and grudging acknowledgment.

1/27/1785 University of Georgia Founded
A State Bets on Education Before It Finishes Building Roads

The University of Georgia was founded in January 1785, becoming the first state chartered public university in the United States. The Revolutionary War had ended only a few years earlier, and the new nation was still improvising its institutions. Georgia's legislature concluded that a republic required educated citizens, especially in a frontier state where survival still demanded cooperation from weather, agriculture, and luck. Establishing a university became an act of faith in the future—a gamble that knowledge was a better investment than expanding militias or buying more land.

University of Georgia 1785

Abraham Baldwin, a Yale educated minister and legislator, drafted the charter. He envisioned an institution rooted in Enlightenment ideals, offering education to young men who would become leaders in law, medicine, politics, and the emerging civic life of the state. The decision to create a publicly funded university reflected a growing belief that education should not be restricted to wealth or lineage. Baldwin argued that learning was essential to maintaining liberty, a claim that resonated even in a region where formal schooling remained rare.

The university's actual construction lagged behind its founding. It would be years before classes were held and decades before the campus resembled anything grander than clustered buildings surrounded by wilderness. Yet its presence signaled a shift. Georgia joined the larger American vision that valued intellectual development as a foundation of national growth. The university's early curriculum combined classical studies with practical instruction, preparing students for a society rebuilding itself from revolution.

As the nineteenth century progressed, the University of Georgia grew in size, scope, and ambition. It weathered the Civil War, Reconstruction, and social upheaval. Eventually, it expanded access to women and people of color, reflecting broader national struggles toward equality. Its transformation mirrored the country's own—uneven, contested, and ultimately forward moving.

Today the university stands as a major public institution, far removed from the modest plan scribbled on parchment in 1785. But the founding decision remains instructive: even in unstable times, investing in education is a declaration that the future deserves preparation rather than improvisation.

Takeaway: The University of Georgia's founding showed that a young republic understood a simple truth, a democracy works better when its citizens can read the laws they're defending.

1/14/1784 U.S. CONGRESS RATIFIES PARIS TREATY
THE REVOLUTION ENDS OFFICIALLY, EVEN IF MEMORY INSISTS ON DRAMATIZING IT

Congress ratified the Treaty of Paris on 14 January 1784, formally ending the American Revolutionary War. Fighting had ceased in 1781 after Yorktown, but without ratification the war remained legally unresolved. Diplomats negotiated throughout 1782 and 1783, shaping terms that recognized American independence, established borders, and addressed fishing rights, property claims, and the delicate task of disentangling two nations that had once been one.

The treaty required ratification within six months of signing. Congress, operating under the Articles of Confederation, struggled to gather enough delegates for a quorum. Travel was slow, winter unpredictable, and national cohesion tenuous. When enough members finally assembled in Annapolis, they approved the treaty unanimously. The date marked the moment when the Revolution transitioned from battlefield memory to diplomatic fact.

The treaty's provisions reflected compromise. Britain accepted American independence and withdrew troops. The United States agreed to honor debts and address Loyalist property claims—promises that would prove uneven in fulfillment. The borders established in the treaty stretched from the Atlantic to the Mississippi, granting the new nation vast territory it had neither the population nor infrastructure to manage. Western settlement would ignite conflicts with Native nations, foreshadowing expansionist policies the founders barely understood.

1784 Proclamation of the ratification of the Treaty of Paris by the Congress

Ratification did not resolve the political fragility of the new republic. The Articles of Confederation offered limited national authority, prompting economic instability and interstate tension. But the treaty gave the United States what it needed most: legitimacy. Recognition by Britain, still the world's dominant power, signaled to other nations that the United States was not a rebellious province but a sovereign state.

The day passed without grand ceremony. Congress moved on to routine matters, reflecting a country already adjusting to self-governance. But the treaty's ratification remains a quiet milestone, the administrative signature that officially closed the door on colonial status.

Takeaway: Ratifying the Treaty of Paris proved that revolutions end not with fireworks but with paperwork, and that independence becomes real only when recognized in ink.

1/15/1559 Elizabeth I Crowned
A Monarchy in Crisis Receives Its Most Capable Survivor

Elizabeth I, late 1580s

Elizabeth I was crowned on 15 January 1559, inheriting a kingdom fractured by religious conflict, political instability, and years of abrupt policy reversals. Her father, Henry VIII, had torn England from Rome. Her brother, Edward VI, strengthened

Protestant reforms. Her sister, Mary I, tried to restore Catholicism with fire and force. By the time Elizabeth reached the throne, the nation was exhausted by whiplash.

Elizabeth's coronation offered relief. She possessed political instinct, careful restraint, and a sharp sense of presentation. Her legitimacy remained questioned by Catholic powers who considered her birth illegitimate, yet she navigated diplomatic hostility with patience. She restored Protestantism while avoiding the extremes of her siblings, adopting a settlement that stabilized religious life without satisfying either side fully. Compromise became her strength.

Her reign ushered in what later writers called the Elizabethan Era—a period marked by exploration, cultural flourishing, and political consolidation. Figures like Shakespeare, Marlowe, and Spenser thrived. Adventurers such as Drake and Raleigh expanded English maritime ambition. At home, Elizabeth strengthened central authority without drifting into autocracy, relying on trusted advisors while keeping potential rivals in check through strategic ambiguity.

The greatest test came from Spain. Philip II's Armada sailed in 1588 with the intention of restoring Catholic control. The English fleet, aided by weather and tactical advantage, repelled the invasion. The victory reshaped European power dynamics and solidified Elizabeth's reputation.

Her personal life became legend: the "Virgin Queen," unmarried and symbolically wedded to the nation. Whether this choice stemmed from prudence, independence, or political necessity remains debated. But it preserved her authority and prevented foreign princes from gaining influence.

Elizabeth ruled for forty-four years, leaving England stronger, richer, and more cohesive than she found it. She stabilized a country teetering on division and positioned it to become a major European power.

Takeaway: Elizabeth's coronation proved that effective leadership requires steadiness after chaos, and that sometimes the most powerful act is refusing to let others define your rule.

1/26/1950 INDIA BECOMES A REPUBLIC
A DEMOCRACY ASSERTS ITS FULL INDEPENDENCE WITH INK, INSTITUTION, AND AMBITION

India became a republic on 26 January 1950 when its new constitution took effect, replacing the British crown's authority with a sovereign democratic framework. Although India had gained independence in 1947, the nation initially retained a British monarch as symbolic head of state. Adopting the constitution ended that transitional arrangement and established the Republic of India under President Rajendra Prasad.

First Cabinet of India

The constitution, drafted under the leadership of B.R. Ambedkar, was among the most comprehensive in history. It blended democratic principles, federal structure, fundamental rights, and protection for historically marginalized communities. Its creation required reconciling linguistic diversity, religious plurality, and regional interests across a subcontinent fractured by colonial rule and partition trauma.

Republic Day symbolized renewal. It marked India's transition from colony to constitutional democracy, asserting sovereignty through law rather than lineage. The nation embraced universal adult suffrage, granting voting rights to hundreds of millions regardless of caste, gender, or wealth—truly a democratic expansion unprecedented in scale.

Challenges remained enormous. Poverty, illiteracy, sectarian tensions, and economic disparity threatened unity. Yet the Constitution provided a framework that survived coups, wars, political upheavals, and social transformation. India's democratic continuity, while imperfect, stands as one of its most significant achievements.

Republic Day celebrations highlight both pride and paradox: a nation still grappling with inherited inequalities while maintaining one of the world's largest democratic systems.

Takeaway: India's republic status proved that independence becomes real only when a nation writes its own rules and agrees to live by them.

1/29/1861 KANSAS ADMITTED AS A FREE STATE
A HARD-FOUGHT ENTRY THAT EXPOSED THE NATION'S DEEPENING FRACTURES

Kansas became the thirty fourth U.S. state on 29 January 1861, admitted as a free state after a seven-year stretch of violence, political sabotage, and ideological trench warfare known collectively as "Bleeding Kansas". What Congress had advertised as an experiment in democratic choice, letting settlers vote on whether slavery would be permitted, collapsed under the weight of national obsession. Pro-slavery advocates flooded into the territory from Missouri. Anti-slavery settlers arrived armed with conviction and, increasingly, with rifles. The ballot box became a battlefield years before Fort Sumter, and when Kansas finally entered as a free state, just two and a half months before the war's opening shots—the country's fracture was no longer theoretical.

The Kansas Nebraska Act of 1854 had been sold as a compromise. It was nothing of the sort. As it dismantled the Missouri Compromise line that had tried, however inadequately, to contain slavery's expansion. Instead, it invited both sides to contest the territory's future through population, pressure, or merely brute force. Fraudulent elections became routine. Atrocities multiplied. Two rival governments emerged, each claiming legitimacy. Washington pretended the situation could be resolved through additional paperwork, but the territory was already functioning as a microcosm of what became a breakdown at the national level.

John Brown's raids demonstrated the depth of the crisis. His assault at Pottawatomie Creek and later actions escalated violence from political conflict into moral confrontation. Brown believed slavery was a sin requiring direct intervention, and Kansas became his proving ground. Pro slavery militias retaliated with equal brutality. Towns were burned. Families were displaced. Militancy became expectation rather than exception.

Congress debated Kansas's status with growing exhaustion. The battle had begun in 1855 when free-state settlers drafted the Topeka Constitution and sought admission, only to be blocked by pro-slavery majorities in Congress. Each proposed constitution that followed, Lecompton, Leavenworth, and Wyandotte, reflected clashing visions of the nation's various identities.

Only when southern states began to secede did the stalemate break. Those states departure removed enough pro slavery votes from Congress to admit Kansas as a free state. The timing was quite symbolic. The nation's fracture had become visible, and Kansas entered the Union not as evidence of reconciliation but as confirmation that compromise had failed entirely.

Kansas's admission did not calm tensions. It clarified and grew them. The idea that popular sovereignty could settle the slavery question died in the territory's burned houses and disputed ballots. The deeper truth emerged plainly: a moral contradiction of this scale could not be solved by negotiation, vote counts, or half measures. It would be settled by war.

Takeaway: Kansas statehood proved that issues rooted in moral contradiction cannot be negotiated indefinitely, and that once violence becomes the language of politics, ballots lose all authority except as preludes to conflict.

CLOSING REFLECTIONS

January does not produce beginnings because history resets itself, it produces them because delay becomes more expensive than action. The events in this chapter share no ideology or geography, but they converge at the same pressure point, systems abandoning inefficiency in favor of structure. Australia organized itself to function. India formalized democracy at unprecedented scale. Haiti seized freedom without permission. Kansas demonstrated that compromise collapses when moral contradiction becomes violence. Even administrative acts, taxes, treaties, universities, followed the same logic, survival through organization. These moments were not romantic or accidental, they were decisions made when existing arrangements stopped working. January marks the calendar point where humans stop arguing about whether change is necessary and start deciding what kind of order will replace failure.

CHAPTER 2

Turning Points in Human Rights & Justice

POWER CLAIMED, POWER BROKEN, POWER ANSWERED

This chapter examines the moments when power meets resistance and discovers it is not as durable as it believed. Each event included here marks a break in the expected order: a decree that redefines a nation's war, a peasant girl who upends military logic, a monk who fractures the largest religious institution in the West, a massacre that exposes the fragility of an empire, a king who learns that legitimacy is a negotiation rather than a birthright, and a genocide that demonstrates how far ideology can descend when no restraints remain. These moments do not sit comfortably together, but they share a structural truth: human rights and justice emerge only when people stop accepting the conditions imposed on them.

The forces at work in this chapter are not subtle. They involve states using violence to preserve control, and individuals or populations refusing to cooperate with systems that no longer deserve obedience. They reveal how rapidly authority collapses once its moral foundation erodes. Nobody expected Joan of Arc to shift the trajectory of a war. Nobody expected Martin Luther to destabilize Europe with a hammer and a list. Nobody expected enslaved people to transform the Civil War's purpose by stepping across Union lines and insisting on agency. Nobody expected ordinary Russians marching with icons to trigger the first tremor of revolution. Yet each episode shows how quickly the balance changes when the governed decide they will no longer participate in their own subordination.

These stories clarify a simple pattern. Justice is never granted from above. It is forced into existence when people, whether through defiance, survival, conviction, or truth telling, refuse to permit the continuation of what power has normalized. Sometimes the shift is immediate. Sometimes it takes decades. Sometimes it happens only after catastrophe makes denial impossible. But once the break occurs, the old structure does not recover. It can only be replaced, revised, or dismantled entirely.

Life Lesson: Systems built on domination endure only as long as people agree to them; once that agreement ends, justice begins to take their place.

1/1/1863 EMANCIPATION PROCLAMATION TAKES EFFECT
A WARTIME DECREE TURNS REBELLION INTO REVOLUTION

On 1 January 1863 Abraham Lincoln's Emancipation Proclamation came into force, transforming the Civil War from a struggle over secession into a battle over human freedom. The document did not end slavery outright. It targeted only those states in

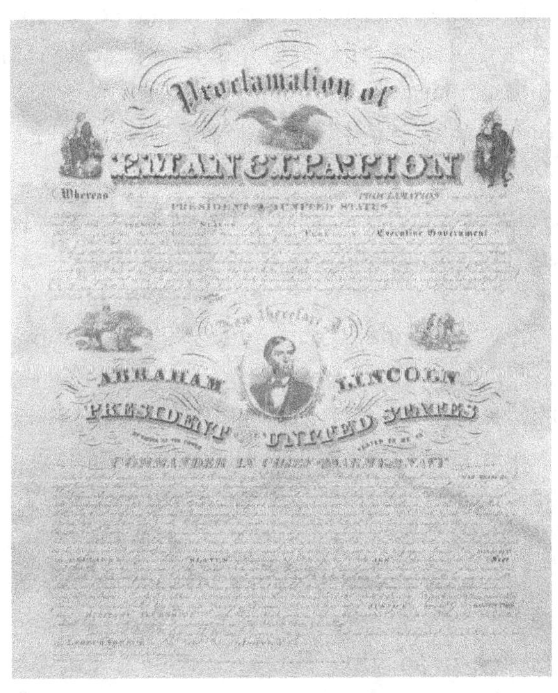

rebellion, declaring enslaved people in Confederate territory "forever free." It was both limited and seismic, a wartime measure crafted to weaken the Confederacy while redefining the Union's moral purpose.

Lincoln had hesitated for months. He understood that any declaration involving slavery risked alienating border states whose loyalty was essential. But as the war dragged on, casualties mounted, and the conflict's political logic shifted. The Union needed a strategic advantage. Depriving the Confederacy of its enslaved labor force offered one. Opening the army to

Black enlistment offered another. The proclamation promised both.

When the order took effect, celebrations erupted in abolitionist strongholds while confusion spread across Confederate territory. Some enslaved people fled immediately toward Union lines. Others waited for advancing troops. Enforcement depended entirely on military success. Freedom traveled at the pace of the army, not the pen. Yet the psychological shock was immediate. The Confederacy understood it now fought not only for independence but for the preservation of slavery. The stakes hardened on both sides.

Black men enlisted in large numbers, filling regiments that would prove decisive in later campaigns. Their service undercut every argument claiming they were unfit for citizenship. The war's moral center shifted. Foreign powers reconsidered recognizing the Confederacy, unwilling to align with a slaveholding rebellion once the Union's objective became emancipation.

The proclamation's limitations were obvious. It did not free enslaved people in Union held areas. It did not abolish slavery nationally. But it changed the direction of the war irreversibly. It prepared the ground for the Thirteenth Amendment, which would finally outlaw slavery everywhere in 1865.

Lincoln's decree redefined the nation's meaning even before it redefined its laws. The United States, inconsistent in its principles since birth, committed itself formally to ending the institution that had shaped its economy, politics, and contradictions. The proclamation was not the end of slavery, but it was the beginning of slavery's collapse.

Takeaway: The Emancipation Proclamation proved that a single declaration cannot finish a struggle, but it can change the terms so completely that the old order never recovers.

1/3/1521 MARTIN LUTHER EXCOMMUNICATED
A MONK'S ARGUMENTS OUTGROW THE CHURCH'S PATIENCE

On 3 January 1521, Pope Leo X excommunicated Martin Luther, ending months of escalating tension between the Catholic Church and a German monk who had become its most relentless critic. Luther's Ninety five Theses, posted in 1517, challenged the sale of indulgences and questioned the authority of Church hierarchy. What began as theological dispute evolved into a continent wide upheaval as Luther's ideas spread through pamphlets, sermons, and the newly energized printing presses.

Luther refused to recant. Rome responded with increasing pressure, culminating in the papal bull "Decet Romanum Pontificem", which formally expelled him from the Church. Excommunication was intended to silence him. Instead, it liberated him. Freed from ecclesiastical obedience, Luther accelerated his reform efforts, translating the Bible into German and urging princes to restructure religious life according to scripture rather than papal decree.

The Church viewed his defiance as a threat to unity and authority. For centuries, it had maintained a monopoly on interpretation and doctrine. Luther's insistence that individuals could read scripture directly and that salvation came through faith alone undermined institutional power. The conflict widened into a political struggle as German princes saw an opportunity to assert independence from Rome.

Excommunication did not end the story; it escalated it. Months later, Luther appeared before the Diet of Worms, where he delivered the declaration that he could not recant without betraying conscience and scripture. The divide hardened into the Protestant Reformation, reshaping European faith, politics, and social structure.

Luther (right) meeting Cardinal Cajetan (left)

The consequences rippled outward for centuries. Nations aligned according to confessional lines. Wars erupted. Education systems changed. The relationship between church and state fractured and evolved. Luther's break with Rome altered Western civilization, proving that one monk with a pen and a stubborn conviction could ignite transformations that institutions could not contain.

Takeaway: Luther's excommunication showed that banning a voice can amplify it, and that revolutions often begin when a single dissenter refuses to accept the script handed down to him.

1/6/1412 JOAN OF ARC BORN TO SAVE FRANCE
A PEASANT GIRL ENTERS HISTORY WITHOUT ASKING PERMISSION

January 6th is widely used as the date to celebrate the birthday of Joan of Arc. It is accepted that the year of her birth was 1412 and the town of the event was Domrémy. It is a small village that had no reason to expect it was raising France's future military catalyst. The Hundred Years' War had fractured the kingdom, demoralized its armies, and left the French crown wobbling between defeat and irrelevance. Into this landscape stepped a teenage peasant who claimed divine instruction and possessed a resolve that made seasoned commanders appear hesitant.

Joan's visions instructed her to drive out the English and escort the Dauphin Charles to his coronation. In any other era, such claims would have ended the story immediately. But France was desperate. Rumor, prophecy, and morale mattered almost as much as military strategy. When Joan arrived at court in 1429, she overcame enough skepticism to be taken seriously, examined, questioned, and ultimately allowed to proceed.

Given armor, a banner, and an unconventional, largely symbolic command, Joan transformed from curiosity into force multiplier. At Orléans, she revitalized a demoralized army, pressing for bold assaults that broke the English siege. Her presence electrified French troops and unsettled opponents. Victories followed with startling speed. Soon after, she accompanied Charles to Reims, securing his coronation as King Charles VII. The symbolic victory reshaped the war's momentum.

Joan's rise also made her a political liability. Rival factions distrusted her influence, and her usefulness did not guarantee protection. In 1430 she was captured by Burgundian forces allied with England, sold to the English, and put on trial for heresy. The proceedings were less about theology and more about discrediting the crown she had helped legitimize. She was condemned and executed in 1431 at age nineteen.

Her death failed to erase her impact. Decades later, the Church nullified her trial, acknowledging its political nature. France elevated her to patriot and martyr. Centuries afterward, she became a saint, a national symbol, and a reminder that conviction can disrupt hierarchies long before institutions realize what is happening.

Takeaway: Joan of Arc's story shows that history does not always move through rank or permission, and that belief, when aligned with timing and pressure, can outmaneuver entire power structures.

1/15/1929 BIRTH OF MARTIN LUTHER KING JR.
A PREACHER'S SON ARRIVES IN A COUNTRY THAT WILL ONE DAY NEED HIS VOICE

Martin Luther King Jr. was born on 15 January 1929 in Atlanta, Georgia, into a world structured by segregation and sustained by laws designed to keep Black Americans politically silent and economically constrained. His birth attracted no national attention; he entered a society where Black children inherited obstacles long before they learned to name them. But the household he entered—anchored by faith, education, and community leadership—would shape a mind capable of challenging the deepest injustices in American life.

King's father, a pastor, provided an environment steeped in activism and moral clarity. The Black church served as both sanctuary and organizing center, a place where sermons doubled as survival strategies. Jim Crow laws, lynching, and racial violence created a climate where dignity had to be defended daily. King absorbed these realities, and the contradictions of a nation preaching liberty while practicing segregation became early lessons that would later inform his life's work.

Though his birth date now symbolizes a turning point in American moral history, King's path to national leadership was not predetermined. He excelled academically, skipped grades, and entered college young. His theological training blended scholarship with a developing philosophy of nonviolence influenced by African American tradition, Christian ethics, and the teachings of Gandhi. By the time he accepted a pastorate in Montgomery, Alabama, he possessed not only rhetorical talent but an intellectual foundation capable of sustaining a national movement.

Within a few years, the Montgomery Bus Boycott thrust King into prominence. His calm defiance, strategic discipline, and moral reasoning distinguished him in a movement filled with courageous leaders. His birth had placed him at the tail end of the 1920s; his rise positioned him at the center of the twentieth century's defining struggle.

King's influence extended far beyond civil rights legislation. He confronted economic injustice, militarism, and the nation's moral direction. He challenged not only laws but the American conscience. Yet his journey began in a segregated hospital room during a year when the Great Depression loomed and racial inequality was an unchallenged fact. The child born that day would grow into a man who insisted that moral progress required confrontation, sacrifice, and unrelenting hope.

Takeaway: King's birth proved that transformative leaders often arrive quietly, and that history sometimes depends on a child born into the very injustice he will spend his life dismantling.

1/20/1265 FIRST ENGLISH PARLIAMENT CONVENES
A KING'S POLITICAL GAMBLE BECOMES A CORNERSTONE OF REPRESENTATIVE GOVERNMENT

The first English Parliament convened in January 1265 under the direction of Simon de Montfort, who had seized control of the government during a rebellion against King Henry III. Medieval England was still an experiment in balancing royal authority with baronial power. De Montfort, needing legitimacy and support, summoned not only nobles and clergy—as was customary—but also elected burgesses from towns. It was a radical act: commoners invited into national governance.

England had earlier councils, but none resembling a representative body. De Montfort's assembly offered political voice to merchants, tradesmen, and urban leaders, signaling that taxation and national policy required broader consent. The goal was practical: strengthen de Montfort's position in a civil war he was struggling to control. Yet the precedent he set outlived him.

The 1265 Parliament debated reforms, grievances, and the relationship between crown and subjects. Though short-lived, it reframed governance. Political legitimacy no longer flowed exclusively downward from monarchs but upward from those asked to fund the kingdom. The experiment collapsed months later when de Montfort died in battle, and Henry III reclaimed authority. But the idea took root. Future kings summoned representative bodies with increasing regularity, recognizing that parliaments eased taxation and stabilized governance.

Over centuries, Parliament evolved into a permanent institution, expanding membership, authority, and influence. The House of Commons emerged as a counterweight to monarchy, shaping laws, budgets, and eventually the very foundation of constitutional rule. England's political trajectory—civil wars, reforms, revolutions—centered on defending or expanding parliamentary power.

The gathering in 1265 was not a fully democratic breakthrough. But it initiated a tradition of representation that reshaped political systems worldwide. The principle that government requires participation from governed communities began here, in a moment of necessity that became enduring political architecture.

Takeaway: The first Parliament proved that representation often begins as improvisation, and that once common people enter government, removing them becomes nearly impossible.

1/21/1793 EXECUTION OF LOUIS XVI
A MONARCHY ENDS AT THE GUILLOTINE AFTER RUNNING OUT OF ILLUSIONS AND TIME

Louis XVI was executed on 21 January 1793 in Paris, his death marking the definitive overthrow of the French monarchy. The Revolution, which began in 1789, had dismantled the institutions supporting royal power, but the king's fate remained uncertain. Some favored constitutional monarchy; others demanded accountability for centuries of privilege. A series of misjudgments sealed Louis's demise: his resistance to reform, his attempted escape in 1791, and his secret dealings with foreign powers.

Execution of Louis XVI

When evidence emerged that Louis had conspired with Austria and Prussia, revolutionaries concluded he posed an existential threat to the new republic. Put on trial as "Citizen Capet," he faced charges of treason. The National Convention voted for execution by narrow margins, revealing a nation divided but determined to eliminate the risk of royal restoration.

Louis faced the guillotine in the Place de la Révolution, climbed the scaffold, and attempted to speak, but drums drowned his final words. The blade fell, and the crowd erupted. His execution shocked Europe, provoking outrage among monarchies and admiration among radicals. France's revolution now stood unmistakably apart from compromise: the old order was not being reformed—it was being removed.

The king's death intensified internal divisions and external threats. The Revolution soon descended into the Reign of Terror, where suspicion and ideological purity fueled mass executions. Yet Louis's execution ensured that monarchy would not return on familiar terms. Even when Napoleon crowned himself Emperor, he did so with a revised relationship to legitimacy—one built on military achievement rather than divine right.

Louis XVI's fall became a symbol of political transformation. The guillotine, now infamous, represented the Revolution's belief that sovereignty resided in the people, not the monarch.

Takeaway: Louis XVI's execution proved that revolutions do not negotiate with symbols of the old world, and that once a king loses moral authority, the throne becomes just another chair.

1/22/1905 BLOODY SUNDAY IN RUSSIA
A PEACEFUL MARCH MEETS GUNFIRE AND IGNITES A REVOLUTION'S FIRST SPARKS

Bloody Sunday occurred on 22 January 1905, 9 January by the Russian calendar, when thousands of Russian workers marched toward the Winter Palace in St Petersburg carrying petitions rather than weapons. Led by Georgy Gapon, the procession demanded shorter hours, fair wages, and political reform. The demonstrators believed Nicholas II would hear their grievances if they approached peacefully. They carried icons, sang hymns, and brought their families. They expected an audience. They received gunfire.

Imperial troops, tense and unevenly commanded, opened fire on the crowd. Panic followed. At least hundreds were killed, possibly more, and thousands were wounded. News of the massacre spread rapidly across the empire, shattering the image of the Tsar as a benevolent ruler ignorant of his people's suffering. Whether through direct responsibility or absence, he now appeared complicit or indifferent. The bond between ruler and ruled fractured in a single winter afternoon.

Bloody Sunday ignited a wave of unrest. Strikes swept major cities, uprisings flared in rural regions, and mutinies broke out within the military. The year 1905 became a prolonged crisis rather than a single revolt. Workers organized councils known as soviets, improvised bodies that foreshadowed the political structures of later revolutions. Demands expanded quickly, moving beyond workplace grievances toward constitutional limits on autocratic power.

Under sustained pressure, Nicholas II issued the October Manifesto, promising civil liberties and establishing the Duma, a legislative assembly nominally meant to share authority with the monarchy. The concession was tactical. When the Duma challenged imperial authority, the Tsar dissolved it repeatedly, rewriting electoral rules and hollowing out reform. The measures bought time, not trust.

"Bloody Sunday" in Russia 1905

Bloody Sunday did not end the Romanov dynasty, but it exposed its weakness. When the revolutions of 1917 erupted, they drew directly from the grievances, structures, and disillusionment first revealed in 1905. The massacre became remembered as the moment many Russians concluded that the autocracy would not protect them, and that reform offered from above was a controlled illusion.

Takeaway: Bloody Sunday proved that once a government turns its weapons on its own people, legitimacy does not recover through concessions. It waits to be replaced.

1/27/2025 Holocaust Remembrance Day Declared

A Global Reckoning with the Darkest Machinery of Human Cruelty

International Holocaust Remembrance Day marks 27 January 1945, when Soviet forces liberated Auschwitz-Birkenau, the largest and most infamous Nazi extermination camp. The gates opened onto a landscape of starvation, ash, and industrialized murder. Survivors emerged skeletal, traumatized, and uncertain whether the world would believe what they had endured. Liberation exposed the scale of genocide the Nazis had hidden behind euphemisms, bureaucracy, and barbed wire.

The Holocaust was not improvisation. It was engineered. Six million Jews were murdered through shootings, ghettos, forced labor, starvation, deportation, gas chambers, and calculated brutality. Alongside them, millions of Roma, disabled individuals, political dissidents, homosexuals, prisoners of war, and others were targeted. The machinery worked because ideology fused with administration. Ordinary functionaries processed extraordinary evil.

After the war, photographs, testimonies, and physical evidence dismantled the Nazis' lies. Trials at Nuremberg documented crimes with legal precision. Survivors, often dismissed or doubted, insisted on telling the truth. Remembrance Day exists because memory demanded structure; without it, the temptation to look away becomes too easy.

Today, the anniversary forces nations to confront not only history but the conditions that produced it: dehumanization, conspiracy myths, authoritarianism, and indifference. Auschwitz was not an accident. It was the culmination of hatred left unchecked.

Takeaway: Holocaust remembrance proves that memory is a responsibility, and that forgetting is the first step toward repetition.

1/30/1948 ASSASSINATION OF MAHATMA GANDHI
A NATION LOSES THE CONSCIENCE THAT GUIDED ITS STRUGGLE FOR FREEDOM

Mahatma Gandhi was assassinated on 30 January 1948 in New Delhi by Nathuram Godse, a Hindu nationalist enraged by Gandhi's insistence on nonviolence, unity, and reconciliation between Hindus and Muslims. India had gained independence only months earlier, but the triumph was overshadowed by the horrors of partition—mass migration, communal violence, and political uncertainty. Gandhi worked to calm tensions, traveling between volatile regions and refusing food during riots until combatants stepped back from brutality.

His assassination shocked India. Crowds flooded the streets. The man who had confronted empire with moral force, fasted to prevent bloodshed, and demanded justice for all communities was killed not by an imperial power but by someone from his own country. The tragedy underscored the volatility of a nation struggling to stabilize after colonial rule.

Gandhi's philosophy of nonviolence—rooted in truth, discipline, and moral clarity—became a global model for civil rights movements. His death elevated him further, transforming his life into a symbol of resistance against injustice. But for India in 1948, the loss was immediate and devastating. A divided nation lost the one figure who could challenge both state violence and sectarian hatred with equal authority.

Takeaway: Gandhi's assassination proved that moral leadership is both powerful and vulnerable, and that even the strongest movements can lose their anchor in a single moment of fanaticism.

1/31/1865 THIRTEENTH AMENDMENT PASSED BY CONGRESS

A NATION FINALLY OUTLAWS THE INSTITUTION IT SPENT EIGHTY YEARS DEFENDING, COMPROMISING OVER, AND GOING TO WAR ABOUT

Congress passed the Thirteenth Amendment on 31 January 1865, abolishing slavery throughout the United States and ending the legal foundation of an institution that had shaped American economics, politics, and moral hypocrisy since before independence. The vote was 119 to 56 in the House—narrow enough that Abraham Lincoln had to deploy every political tool available, including patronage, persuasion, and promises he may or may not have intended to keep. The amendment did not end racism, inequality, or the systems built to preserve white supremacy. But it did eliminate the legal right to own human beings, which turned out to be a necessary first step even if subsequent steps took another century and remain incomplete.

Slavery had been the nation's original sin and its most profitable compromise. The Constitution never used the word "slave" but embedded protections for the institution in multiple clauses, ensuring Southern states would ratify and Northern merchants could profit from the trade. Decades of political gymnastics—the Missouri Compromise, the Compromise of 1850, the Kansas-Nebraska Act—attempted to manage slavery's expansion without addressing its existence. The strategy failed spectacularly. By 1861, the country was at war with itself, and by 1865, slavery's abolition had become militarily necessary, morally unavoidable, and politically achievable only through a constitutional amendment that required twisting enough arms to dislocate shoulders.

The amendment's passage was not inevitable. Lincoln's Emancipation Proclamation in 1863 had freed enslaved people in

Confederate territory—a wartime measure with dubious legal permanence. Once the war ended, the proclamation's authority would become questionable. A constitutional amendment offered certainty. It would enshrine abolition in the nation's founding document, making slavery's elimination irreversible through normal political processes.

But constitutional amendments require a two-thirds majority in both chambers of Congress and ratification by three-fourths of the states. The Senate had passed the amendment in April 1864 with votes to spare. The House rejected it in June, falling short by thirteen votes. Lincoln, despite his reputation for moral clarity, understood that moral clarity without votes was just rhetoric. He needed the amendment passed before the war ended and before a restored South could rejoin Congress and block it indefinitely.

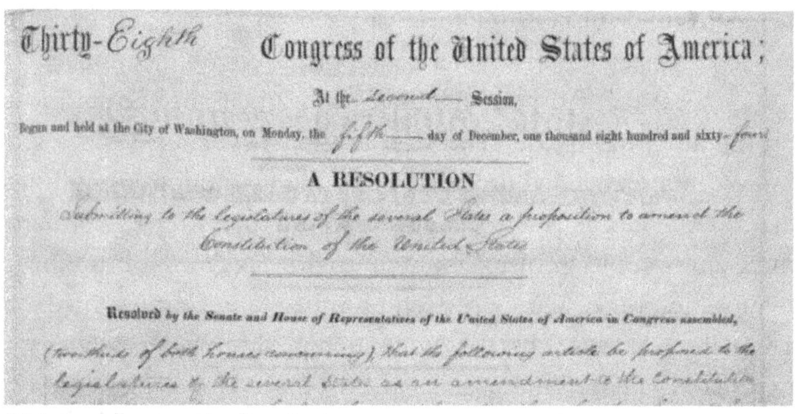

13th Amendment to the Constitution

Lincoln's re-election in November 1864 provided momentum. Sherman's march through Georgia demonstrated the war was ending with Union victory. Lame-duck Democrats, defeated in the election but still holding seats until March, faced a choice: vote for abolition now or let history remember them as the final defenders of slavery. Lincoln applied pressure expertly.

Federal jobs were offered. Lame-duck congressmen were promised positions. Wavering representatives received visits from administration officials who explained, with varying degrees of subtlety, that cooperation would be rewarded and obstruction remembered.

The vote on 31 January was tense. Galleries packed with spectators. The count proceeded slowly as each representative announced their position. When the total reached 119—two votes more than required—the chamber erupted. Members cheered. Spectators wept. Some Democrats walked out rather than participate in the celebration. Lincoln, watching from the White House, received the news and quietly acknowledged that the amendment's passage secured what the war had been fought to achieve, even if many who fought it had not initially understood that goal.

The amendment's language was deceptively simple: "Neither slavery nor involuntary servitude, except as a punishment for crime whereof the party shall have been duly convicted, shall exist within the United States, or any place subject to their jurisdiction." Twenty-seven words that abolished an institution but included an exception—convict labor—that would later enable new forms of forced servitude under the guise of criminal justice. Southern states, once they ratified the amendment under Reconstruction pressure, immediately exploited that loophole through Black Codes, convict leasing, and mass incarceration systems designed to replicate slavery's labor dynamics without its explicit legal structure.

The Thirteenth Amendment transformed the United States from a slaveholding republic into a nation where slavery was constitutionally prohibited. That transformation was monumental, overdue, and incomplete. It eliminated the legal category of "slave" but did not eliminate the racial hierarchies, economic exploitation, and social systems built to maintain those hierarchies. Sharecropping, Jim Crow laws, segregation, disenfranchisement, and systematic violence replaced slavery with new mechanisms of control that preserved many of slavery's outcomes without its formalities.

Still, the amendment mattered. It codified a moral principle into law, making abolition permanent and establishing a foundation for future civil rights progress. The Fourteenth and Fifteenth Amendments followed, expanding citizenship and voting rights. Later civil rights movements invoked the Thirteenth Amendment's promise when challenging systems that perpetuated racial oppression. The amendment was not an ending but a beginning—one that acknowledged the nation could no longer pretend slavery was compatible with its stated ideals.

Lincoln did not live to see the amendment ratified. He was assassinated in April, weeks after the war's end and months before the amendment achieved the necessary state approvals. But his role in securing congressional passage ensured that his most significant legacy would be constitutional rather than merely presidential. The amendment outlived him, outlasted Reconstruction, and remained when later generations needed a legal foundation to challenge the systems that replaced slavery.

Takeaway: The Thirteenth Amendment showed that ending slavery required both moral conviction and political force, and that legal abolition was only the beginning of addressing centuries of damage.

CLOSING REFLECTION

Power does not collapse because it is challenged, it collapses because it is exposed. Each event in this chapter shows a system losing authority the moment its justifications stop working. Emancipation reframed a war that could no longer pretend neutrality. Luther shattered institutional monopoly by insisting belief could survive without permission. Joan of Arc proved legitimacy could be claimed from conviction rather than rank. Bloody Sunday revealed an empire willing to fire on its own people rather than listen. In every case, power failed not when opposition grew strong, but when its moral logic broke down in public view. Once that rupture occurred, force could delay change but could not reverse it. Authority survived only where consent remained, and where consent died, replacement became inevitable.

CHAPTER 3

REVOLUTIONS, REBELLIONS, & SOCIAL UPHEAVAL

FAULT LINES THAT FINALLY GIVE WAY

Revolutions and rebellions do not appear out of nowhere. They gather in the background, formed from pressures that institutions dismiss until those pressures can no longer be contained. When change finally breaks open, it looks abrupt only to those who ignored the warning signs. Haiti's uprising, Iran's revolution, America's political awakening, Britain's labor movement, and the collapse of Prohibition all follow the same arc. Systems fail, and the people living within them decide they will not continue participating in their own disadvantage.

These events show how quickly authority dissolves once legitimacy erodes. Empires built on coerced labor discover their strength was borrowed. Monarchies wrapped in ceremony collapse when public patience reaches its limit. Governments claiming moral superiority expose their fragility by policing behavior they cannot control. Economic and political structures that appeared stable unravel when the demands placed on ordinary people exceed what they can or will endure. Each case reveals a basic truth: power functions only with consent, and when that consent evaporates, the governing order loses its anchor.

Revolutions are not graceful. They begin in frustration, escalate through disorder, and end by reshaping society in ways that are rarely predictable. Sometimes they produce progress, sometimes backlash, but the mechanism is constant. Change arrives the moment a population concludes that the old system no longer deserves its compliance, and by the time that realization surfaces, the collapse has already begun.

Life Lesson: Upheaval begins the moment people decide the existing system is no longer worth enduring, and once that decision is made, the old world has already started to fall.

1/1/1959 CUBAN REVOLUTION CONCLUDES
A DICTATOR FLEES AT MIDNIGHT, AND A NEW ONE ARRIVES TO PROMISES NO ONE ASKED HIM TO KEEP

Fulgencio Batista fled Cuba shortly after midnight on 1 January 1959, ending a regime that had grown rich through corruption, gambling revenue, and the reliable American practice of looking the other way when convenient allies behaved badly. His departure was neither dignified nor unexpected. Rebel forces led by Fidel Castro had spent two years fighting their way out of the Sierra Maestra mountains, gaining support as Batista's government collapsed under its own brutality and incompetence. By New Year's Eve, Batista realized the game was finished. He packed what he could carry, boarded a plane, and left the country to whoever wanted it most.

Revolutionary cavalry entering Habana after the triumph of the Revolution

Castro wanted it most.

Within a week, Castro's convoy rolled into Havana amid jubilant crowds who saw liberation rather than the forty-plus years of authoritarian rule that would follow. The revolution promised democracy, land reform, and an end to American domination. It delivered none of those things in the form advertised. What it did deliver was the overthrow of one strongman by another, this time with better rhetoric and a longer beard.

The revolution began modestly enough. Castro and a small group of fighters launched their rebellion in 1953 with an attack on the Moncada Barracks that failed spectacularly. Most were killed or captured. Castro was imprisoned, then exiled to Mexico, where he met Che Guevara and plotted a return. In 1956, they sailed back to Cuba aboard the yacht Granma with eighty-two men. Nearly all were killed or captured immediately. The survivors—fewer than twenty—retreated into the mountains and began a guerrilla campaign that somehow worked.

Batista's regime made it easier. Torture, corruption, and violent suppression alienated the middle class, intellectuals, and peasants alike. The United States continued supporting Batista until it became embarrassing, then quietly shifted toward neutrality as his collapse became inevitable. Castro exploited every misstep, positioning himself as a nationalist reformer rather than the communist revolutionary he would soon reveal himself to be.

When Batista fled, Cuba entered a brief period of euphoria. Political prisoners were released. Batista's officials were put on trial—some fairly, many not. Land redistribution began. Literacy campaigns launched. The early reforms were popular and overdue. But the revolution's direction hardened quickly. Political pluralism evaporated. Dissent became treason. The press was silenced. Elections were postponed indefinitely.

The promised democracy never materialized because Castro decided he preferred control to competition.

The United States responded with hostility, imposing an embargo that would last decades and inadvertently provide Castro with a permanent scapegoat for economic failures. The failed Bay of Pigs invasion in 1961 only strengthened his grip. The Cuban Missile Crisis in 1962 nearly triggered nuclear war, proving that small islands can generate outsized geopolitical nightmares when superpowers decide to use them as chess pieces.

Castro ruled Cuba until 2008, far longer than Batista or anyone else imagined possible. His regime delivered universal healthcare and education while simultaneously imprisoning dissidents, suppressing freedom, and maintaining a system that required periodic Soviet subsidies to avoid collapse. The revolution succeeded in ending American domination but replaced it with Soviet dependence, then Venezuelan aid, then a slow economic stagnation punctuated by propaganda.

The revolution that concluded on New Year's Day 1959 was sold as liberation. What it produced was durability without democracy, stability without freedom, and a leader who outlasted ten American presidents while insisting the revolution was still unfolding. Revolutions rarely deliver what they promise. Cuba's delivered something entirely different, then called it victory for half a century.

Takeaway: Castro's takeover proved that revolutions often replace one authoritarian with another, and that the difference between liberation and dictatorship sometimes depends only on whose promises you believed first.

1/2/1492 FALL OF GRANADA (END OF RECONQUISTA)

EIGHT CENTURIES OF CONFLICT CONCLUDE WITH A SURRENDER, A KEY EXCHANGE, AND THE IMMEDIATE EXPULSION OF EVERYONE WHO MADE THE PLACE INTERESTING

The Emirate of Granada surrendered to Ferdinand and Isabella on 2 January 1492, ending nearly eight hundred years of Muslim rule in Iberia and completing the Reconquista—a centuries-long campaign that had become as much cultural identity as military strategy. Boabdil, the last Nasrid ruler, handed over the keys to the Alhambra palace and rode into exile, reportedly weeping as he looked back at the city. His mother, less sympathetic to theatrics, allegedly told him not to cry like a woman for what he could not defend like a man. It was the kind of exit that gets remembered longer than the actual governance.

The Surrender of Granada by Francisco

The fall of Granada was not a surprise. The emirate had survived as a tributary state for decades, paying Christian kingdoms for the privilege of continued existence. But by the late fifteenth century, Ferdinand and Isabella had unified Castile and Aragon, centralized their authority, and decided that religious uniformity was more valuable than tax revenue. Granada's strategic position and symbolic importance made it the final target. The siege began in 1491. It was methodical, patient, and overwhelmingly one-sided. Boabdil negotiated terms, received safe passage, and left.

The Christian monarchs entered Granada in triumph, planting the cross atop the Alhambra and celebrating the end of Islamic political power in Spain. It was framed as a religious victory, the completion of a holy mission begun centuries earlier. Europe took notice. The Pope sent congratulations. Ferdinand and Isabella commissioned celebrations. Spain had been "reconquered," though calling it reconquest required ignoring that much of the population descending from people who had been there all along, regardless of which flag flew overhead.

The victory's consequences arrived quickly and brutally. Within months, the Alhambra Decree was issued, expelling all Jews who refused conversion. Tens of thousands left, carrying skills, knowledge, and networks that had enriched Spanish intellectual and economic life for centuries. Muslims faced similar pressure. Forced conversions began almost immediately, despite earlier promises of religious tolerance. The Inquisition, already active, intensified its efforts to root out heresy, which conveniently included anyone whose commitment to Christianity seemed insufficiently enthusiastic.

The same year that Granada fell, Christopher Columbus sailed west under Ferdinand and Isabella's sponsorship, funded partly by wealth confiscated from expelled Jews. Spain pivoted from consolidating the peninsula to expanding across oceans, transforming from a regional power into a global empire. The conquest of Granada and the conquest of the Americas were not separate events—they were connected chapters in a narrative of expansion, religious zeal, and the conviction that uniformity was strength.

Culturally, the fall of Granada marked the beginning of Spain's Golden Age and the simultaneous narrowing of its intellectual diversity. The Convivencia—the relatively tolerant coexistence of Muslims, Christians, and Jews that had characterized medieval Iberia—was dismantled in favor of Catholic orthodoxy. Libraries were burned. Scholars fled. Arabic texts were destroyed. What remained was a Spain more unified politically but diminished intellectually.

Granada itself became a monument to the past it had just erased. The Alhambra, one of the Islamic world's architectural masterpieces, was preserved not out of respect but as a trophy. Christian kings added their own structures, but the palace's Moorish beauty persisted, a reminder that the culture Spain expelled had built something it could neither replicate nor fully comprehend.

The Reconquista's completion was celebrated as destiny fulfilled, the restoration of Christian Spain after centuries of occupation. But the narrative required selective memory. Iberia's Muslim period had produced advances in mathematics, astronomy, medicine, and philosophy that shaped European thought. The expulsions and forced conversions threw away centuries of accumulated knowledge because religious purity was deemed more important than intellectual vitality.

Takeaway: Granada's fall proved that victories built on religious uniformity often celebrate the conquest while ignoring everything lost in the process, and that empires expand fastest when they stop tolerating the diversity that once made them worth living in.

73

1/8/1918 Wilson's Fourteen Points Speech
A President Proposes World Peace Through Diplomacy, Then Watches Europe Ignore Most of It

Woodrow Wilson addressed Congress in January of 1918, with a speech outlining fourteen principles for ending World War I and preventing future conflicts. The Fourteen Points promised open diplomacy, freedom of the seas, arms reduction, self-determination for colonized peoples, and the establishment of a League of Nations to arbitrate disputes. It was idealistic, comprehensive, and almost immediately doomed to partial implementation at best.

Wilson believed reasoned diplomacy could replace the old system of secret treaties, imperial ambitions, and balance-of-power calculations that had just produced four years of industrialized slaughter. Europe's victorious powers believed Wilson was naïve.

The speech arrived at a moment when the war's outcome remained uncertain. Russia had collapsed into revolution and withdrawn from the fight, freeing Germany to concentrate forces on the Western Front. American troops were arriving in increasing numbers, but their impact was still building. Wilson's speech aimed to articulate why the United States was fighting—not for territorial gain or imperial expansion, but for a new international order based on justice, transparency, and collective security. It was the kind of moral clarity that sounds better in speeches than in peace conferences.

The Fourteen Points addressed specific grievances that had fueled the war. Secret treaties would be abolished in favor of open diplomacy. Colonial claims would be settled with consideration for the colonized populations—a revolutionary suggestion that Wilson himself would later undermine. National boundaries would be redrawn according to ethnicity and self-determination, ignoring the centuries of mixed populations and competing claims that made clean borders impossible. Belgium would be restored. Alsace-Lorraine returned to France. Poland reestablished. It was a blueprint for remaking Europe based on principles rather than power.

The fourteenth point called for a "general association of nations" to guarantee political independence and territorial integrity, the League of Nations. Wilson believed international cooperation, backed by collective security agreements, could prevent future wars. The concept was bold but fragile, dependent on nations voluntarily surrendering sovereignty to a collective body with no enforcement mechanism beyond moral persuasion and coordinated disapproval.

When the Paris Peace Conference convened in 1919, Wilson discovered that idealism travels poorly. Britain and France had their own priorities: punishing Germany, securing reparations, protecting colonial holdings, and ensuring their own security. The Treaty of Versailles incorporated some of Wilson's points—the League of Nations was established, Poland was recreated, new borders were drawn—but the spirit was punitive rather than conciliatory. Germany was blamed, humiliated, and burdened with reparations that crippled its economy and fueled resentment. The treaty planted seeds for another war rather than preventing one.

Wilson returned home expecting triumph. Instead, he faced a hostile Senate that refused to ratify the treaty or join the League of Nations. Republicans opposed surrendering American sovereignty to an international body. Isolationists feared entanglement in European conflicts. Wilson's refusal to compromise or include senators in negotiations alienated potential allies. He embarked on a nationwide speaking tour to rally public support, suffered a debilitating stroke, and watched his vision collapse. The United States never joined the League, crippling the organization before it began.

The speech's legacy is complicated. Self-determination inspired independence movements across Europe and beyond, but Wilson applied the principle selectively. He supported freedom for European nations while ignoring colonized peoples in Africa, Asia, and the Middle East. His administration segregated the federal government and screened the racist film Birth of a Nation at the White House. Wilson's moral leadership abroad contrasted sharply with his tolerance for oppression at home.

Still, the Fourteen Points established principles that shaped twentieth-century international relations. Open diplomacy, self-determination, and collective security became foundational concepts, even when violated in practice. The United Nations borrowed from the League's structure, learning from its failures. Wilson's vision outlasted his ability to implement it, proving that ideas can endure even when their architects do not.

Takeaway: Wilson's Fourteen Points proved that idealism without power is just a speech, and that the gap between what a president promises and what allies accept can swallow entire world orders whole.

1/13/1893 THE INDEPENDENT LABOUR PARTY FOUNDED

BRITISH WORKERS DECIDE REPRESENTATION REQUIRES MORE THAN POLITE REQUESTS

The Independent Labour Party (ILP) was founded on 13 January 1893 in Bradford, England, during a period when industrial workers had political grievances, but no national party dedicated to addressing them. Existing parties—Conservative and Liberal, offered limited sympathy for factory laborers, miners, and working-class families struggling under long hours, low wages, and hazardous conditions. Trade unions could negotiate, but they could not legislate. The ILP emerged to fill that void, insisting that working people deserved their own political engine rather than the borrowed concern of elites.

Keir Hardie, a former miner turned organizer, became the ILP's first chairman and its most visible voice. He argued that capitalism's structural inequalities required more than incremental reform. Workers needed political power equal to their economic contribution. Hardie's approach blended moral conviction with strategic patience. He understood that a working-class party had to appeal to voters beyond union halls. The ILP's platform included expanded suffrage, improved labor rights, access to education, and social welfare protections that would later become pillars of British policy.

The ILP attracted activists seeking an alternative to the narrow focus of trade union representation. It also alarmed business owners and unsettled traditional politicians who had assumed that working class unrest could be managed without widening democratic influence. The party contested elections but initially struggled to win seats. Britain's political machinery was not built for outsiders. Yet the ILP persisted, building networks, campaigning relentlessly, and shifting public conversations.

The turning point arrived when the ILP helped form the Labour Representation Committee in 1900, the precursor to the modern Labour Party. While the ILP did not become the dominant force within that coalition, its ideological DNA shaped Labour's emergence. The party gradually secured seats challenged the dominance of the Liberal Party, and pushed social reforms into mainstream debate.

The ILP eventually became overshadowed by the Labour Party it helped create, leading to ideological tensions and eventual separation in the 1930s. Yet its legacy endured in Labour's commitment to social welfare, labor protections, and the expansion of democratic opportunity.

The founders of the ILP did not live to see the full impact of their work, but their vision redefined British politics. They proved that working people, organized and persistent, could reshape national priorities.

Takeaway: The ILP's creation showed that political power rarely trickles downward, and that when workers want representation, they must build it themselves rather than wait for charity from above.

1/16/1979 THE SHAH OF IRAN FLEES THE COUNTRY
A MONARCHY COLLAPSES UNDER ITS OWN CONTRADICTIONS

On 16 January 1979, Mohammad Reza Shah Pahlavi left Iran under mounting political unrest, marking the effective end of a monarchy that had ruled for centuries. His departure followed months of demonstrations, strikes, and escalating violence. The Shah, once backed by Western powers as a modernizing force, had lost legitimacy at home. Corruption, repression, and the widening gap between elite privilege and popular hardship fueled a revolution that no security force could contain.

The Shah's modernization efforts transformed Iran's infrastructure, economy, and educational systems but alienated conservative clergy, rural populations, and the urban poor. Political opposition was silenced by the SAVAK intelligence service. Elections were hollow. Oil wealth enriched the state but produced uneven benefits. The Shah's claim to lead Iran into modernity could not mask the authoritarianism underpinning his rule.

By 1978, protests spread from Tehran to provincial cities. Demonstrations grew larger despite violent crackdowns. Religious leaders, students, workers, and intellectuals formed an uneasy coalition united by the goal of ending the monarchy. As pressure mounted, the Shah vacillated between concessions and force, satisfying neither supporters nor opponents.

Ayatollah Ruhollah Khomeini, exiled in France, became the revolution's symbolic center. His recorded speeches circulated secretly, shaping ideology and rallying followers. When the Shah left Iran ostensibly for "medical leave," the vacuum was immediate. Crowds flooded the streets celebrating the monarchy's collapse. Khomeini returned weeks later to immense support, shaping the revolution's outcome and establishing the Islamic Republic.

1977: Mohammad Reza and Farah with New Year's guests King Hussein and President Jimmy Carter

The Shah's departure closed the last chapter of Iran's monarchy and ushered in a turbulent new era defined by religious authority, anti-Western sentiment, and political transformation. The revolution's consequences reshaped Middle Eastern geopolitics and continue to influence global affairs.

Takeaway: The Shah's flight proved that modernization without legitimacy collapses quickly, and that regimes fall not when opposition becomes strong, but when public tolerance finally runs out.

1/16/1786 VIRGINIA STATUTE FOR RELIGIOUS FREEDOM ENACTED
AN IDEA WRITTEN YEARS EARLIER FINALLY BECOMES LAW AND REWIRES AMERICAN LIBERTY

On 16 January 1786, Virginia enacted the Virginia Statute for Religious Freedom, formally severing the link between government power and religious authority. Drafted years earlier by Thomas Jefferson and championed through the legislature by James Madison, the statute declared that belief could not be commanded, taxed, or punished by the state. Faith, it argued, belonged to conscience alone.

The Virginia Statute for Religious Freedom

The law did not arrive gently. Virginia had long supported the Anglican Church through public taxes, and dissenters had faced fines, imprisonment, and social exclusion. The statute dismantled that structure outright. It prohibited compulsory church support, rejected religious tests for public office, and asserted that civil rights did not depend on theological conformity. In plain terms, the government lost the right to tell citizens what to believe.

The argument behind the statute was radical for its time. Jefferson rejected the idea that social order required religious enforcement. Madison went further, warning that state sponsored faith inevitably corrupted both government and religion. Their position infuriated clergy who relied on public funding and alarmed lawmakers who feared moral collapse. None of that stopped the vote.

The statute's passage echoed far beyond Virginia. It provided the intellectual and legal foundation for the First Amendment's guarantees of religious freedom. When the Bill of Rights was drafted a few years later, its language carried the unmistakable imprint of this earlier fight. What had been controversial in one state became a national principle.

Jefferson later insisted the statute be listed among his greatest achievements, alongside authoring the Declaration of Independence and founding the University of Virginia. He notably excluded the presidency. Power, he believed, mattered less than ideas that limited it.

The law did not end religious conflict in America, but it changed its rules permanently. Belief became a private matter, and the state was told to stay in its lane. That separation would be tested repeatedly, but it was never undone.

Takeaway: The Virginia Statute for Religious Freedom proved that revolutions are not only fought on battlefields but won when governments are forced to admit what they have no right to control.

1/16/1919 PROHIBITION RATIFIED
AMERICA OUTLAWS ALCOHOL AND ACCIDENTALLY INVENTS A CRIME BOOM

Prohibition was ratified on 16 January 1919 with the approval of the Eighteenth Amendment, launching a national experiment that aimed to cure society by banning alcohol. Reformers believed intoxication fueled poverty, domestic violence, and moral decay. They expected a sober nation to become a prosperous and peaceful one. The amendment outlawed the manufacture, sale, and transportation of intoxicating liquors; enforcement fell to the Volstead Act. The theory was tidy. Reality was not.

Before Prohibition, alcohol had been woven into American social life. Saloons served as gathering places, political hubs, and relief valves for workers. But they also became symbols of excess and corruption. The temperance movement gained strength through decades of organizing, led by religious activists and women's groups such as the WCTU, who argued that banning alcohol would protect families and uplift society.

Once enacted, the amendment's unintended consequences surfaced quickly. Demand did not disappear. It simply moved underground. Bootlegging operations grew into sophisticated networks. Rumrunners supplied coastal cities. Speakeasies multiplied, hiding behind unmarked doors and coded knocks. Organized crime flourished as syndicates built empires on illegal liquor. Law enforcement became a contest of improvisation. Courts overflowed. Bribery became routine.

Prohibition also divided the country geographically and culturally. Rural, religious communities supported the ban. Urban, immigrant heavy cities resisted it. The law fractured public trust as ordinary citizens routinely violated it. Meanwhile, industrial use of alcohol continued, forcing federal officials to poison denatured alcohol to deter theft—an effort that killed thousands.

Prohibition headline

The amendment achieved few of its moral goals. Alcohol consumption initially dropped, then rebounded. Crime rates rose. Government revenue plunged because liquor taxes had once provided substantial funding. The Great Depression shifted priorities. By 1933, the Twenty First Amendment repealed Prohibition, ending the only constitutional amendment designed to regulate personal behavior nationwide.

In hindsight, Prohibition revealed that legislation cannot reshape human appetite, and moral reform enforced through criminal law often produces more vices than virtues.

Takeaway: Prohibition proved that banning a popular behavior does not eliminate it, and that idealism divorced from reality can transform social problems into criminal enterprises.

CLOSING REFLECTION

Revolutions and upheavals are often remembered as clean turning points, but the events in this chapter expose how uneven and costly they actually are. Haiti's triumph dismantled an empire but inherited isolation and retribution. Iran removed a monarchy only to confront a new concentration of power. Paine's pamphlet pushed the colonies toward independence while opening a long and unresolved debate over the meaning of freedom. Workers built their own political voice, only to watch it absorbed and reshaped by the very system they meant to challenge. Prohibition tried to enforce morality and instead produced a thriving criminal economy. None of these stories offer tidy victories. They demonstrate that when societies break from an old order, they rarely arrive in a cleanly improved one, but in a different landscape that still requires struggle, adjustment, and vigilance to prevent the next cycle of imbalance.

CHAPTER 4

SCIENCE, TECHNOLOGY, & KNOWLEDGE

KNOWLEDGE THAT REFUSES TO STAY STILL

Science and technology advance through the same mechanism, pressure from reality that existing explanations and tools can no longer withstand. Knowledge refuses to stay still because the world refuses to cooperate with comfortable assumptions. Civilizations progress when observation replaces tradition and when systems are rebuilt to match evidence rather than belief.

Science advances by dismantling inherited explanations that no longer hold. Caesar forces time into alignment with mathematics instead of priestly improvisation. Galileo observes Jupiter long enough to see that the heavens do not obey the stories written about them. Shelley imagines the consequences of scientific ambition before most readers understand the science itself. Each moment represents a collision between observation and tradition, and tradition loses every time.

These breakthroughs do not arise from calm or curiosity alone. They emerge when frameworks fail. Earhart tests aviation limits directly in unforgiving conditions because theory alone cannot answer what reality will tolerate. The first Winter Olympics formalize skills rooted in survival rather than sport. Explorer 1 launches under the pressure of national insecurity, yet delivers something more disruptive than reassurance, data that reshapes humanity's understanding of the planet. Science progresses not because people wonder, but because the world refuses to fit inside outdated explanations.

Discovery then hardens into structure. Understanding does not remain abstract. It becomes engineered reality. Technology reshapes the world by altering how people live, move, work, and define what is possible. Each development begins as a response to a concrete problem, measuring time accurately, crossing hostile terrain, building faster machines, preventing catastrophe, communicating across distance, organizing mass movement, or turning isolated events into shared experience. These are not ideas, they are solutions built because existing tools failed.

Engineering is never neutral. The Golden Gate Bridge rewires regional movement. Bentley reshapes expectations of performance and craftsmanship. Apollo 1 and Challenger expose the cost of ignoring system risk, forcing redesigns that save later lives. Radio collapses distance by synchronizing experience. The first newspaper weaponizes information. Ellis Island converts migration into process and policy. Each construction reorganizes society regardless of readiness.

Once built, technology becomes environment. Bridges, networks, vehicles, institutions, and systems define what is normal and what is possible. Human behavior adapts to technology faster than technology adapts to human behavior. Momentum moves in one direction. What begins as a solution becomes a baseline, and future generations inherit outcomes without remembering the uncertainty, risk, and conflict required to create them.

Knowledge expands because someone decides the cost of ignorance is greater than the risk of being wrong. Construction follows because understanding demands embodiment. Science tests reality. Engineering locks the results into the world people must live in.

Life Lesson: Progress occurs when evidence replaces belief and tools replace limitation, and once knowledge is built into the world, neither understanding nor society can return to its previous state.

1/1/44 BC Julian Calendar Introduced
A dictator fixes time with math, priests object accordingly

Julius Caesar introduced the Julian calendar on 1 January 44 BC because Rome's timekeeping system had collapsed into a tangle of ignored rules, political manipulation, and priestly guesswork. The old lunar calendar drifted so far off the seasons that farmers planted crops at the wrong time, festivals arrived months late, and civic planning became a diplomatic exercise in pretending everyone still knew what day it was. Caesar, fresh from reorganizing almost everything else in Rome, decided time itself needed discipline.

He turned to Sosigenes of Alexandria, an astronomer who understood that the solar year—not the moon—offered consistency. The solution was direct: create a calendar of 365 days with an extra day added every fourth year. Rome gained a predictable schedule, and future civilizations inherited a system that would dominate Western timekeeping for more than fifteen centuries.

The adjustment required a one time correction so massive it resembled a cosmic reset. To realign the seasons, Caesar inserted extra days into 46 BC, producing a year so long it earned the nickname the "year of confusion." But once the reset ended, the Julian calendar brought order. Months stabilized. Seasons returned to their proper slots. The Roman state could plan festivals without gambling on lunar cycles. Farmers regained confidence that planting schedules matched the sun, not the guesswork of pontiffs.

Resistance came mostly from traditionalists, especially those who had enjoyed manipulating the old calendar for political advantage. Under the previous system, officials could delay elections or extend terms simply by adjusting the length of the year. Caesar's reform ended that trick. Precision was the enemy of opportunists. But the new system endured because it worked better than anything Rome had used before.

Centuries later, small inaccuracies in the Julian year would accumulate, prompting the Gregorian reform. But for its era, the Julian calendar was a triumph of administrative rationality, a reminder that sometimes progress begins with the simple insistence that days should be counted correctly.

Takeaway: Caesar's calendar showed that even empires need synchronized schedules, and that fixing time requires less mysticism and more arithmetic than most priests preferred.

1/1/1818 First Science Fiction Novel
A Dream of the Future Becomes a Genre with No Intention of Ending

Science fiction's first modern novel arrived in January 1818 under the unlikely title Frankenstein, or The Modern Prometheus. Mary Shelley released it as a gothic experiment, but the book had bigger ambitions than castles and candlelight. It treated science not as background decoration but as the engine of catastrophe, setting a pattern the genre has been riding ever since. Labels struggled to keep up. The ideas did not.

The novel wrestled with creation, responsibility, and intellectual overreach decades before laboratories were public-friendly places. Shelley did not write about ray guns or spaceships. She wrote about what happens when curiosity outruns judgment. Science was not a savior or a villain, it was raw power handed to an unprepared human being.

The book was written in 1816 during the so-called Year Without a Summer, when volcanic ash from Mount Tambora dimmed Europe's skies and forced a group of writers indoors. Boredom, bad weather, and competitive storytelling did the rest. Shelley's idea emerged from conversations about galvanism and whether life could be sparked by human hands. She imagined a scientist assembling a body from dead matter and bringing it to life through unspecified means, then immediately panicking and abandoning the result. The novel is deliberately vague about the mechanics. The moral fallout is anything but.

Shelley treated science as both promise and threat, a duality that would become the backbone of science fiction. Her creature was not born monstrous. It became monstrous through neglect, isolation, and a society that recoiled from what it did not want to understand. The real horror was not animation, but responsibility denied.

As the nineteenth century rolled forward, the book's influence quietly multiplied. Writers borrowed its method, speculation tied to consequence. Industrialization made futures easier to imagine and harder to ignore. By the early twentieth century, Shelley's foundation had expanded into a field large enough to hold utopias, dystopias, alien worlds, and every optimistic or catastrophic invention authors could sketch into existence.

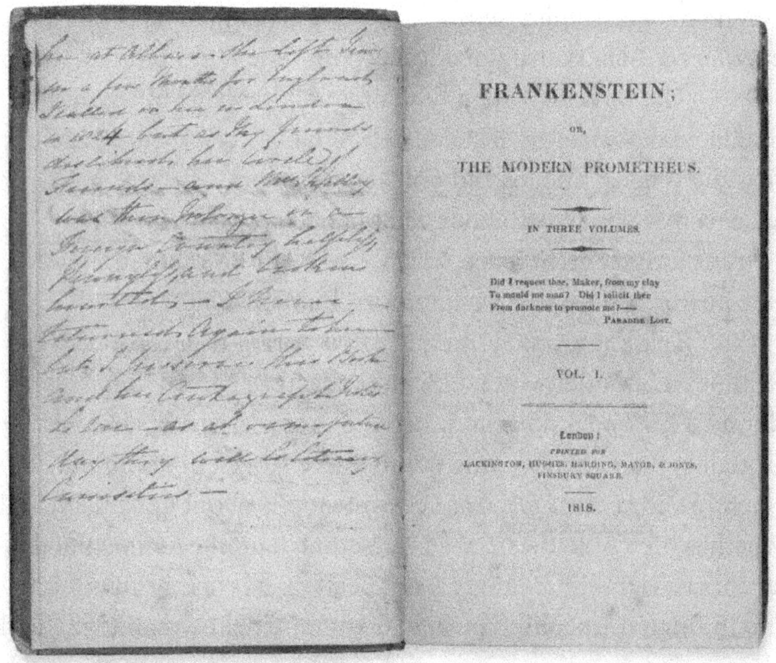

First Print of Frankenstein

Shelley did not set out to invent a genre. She wrote a story about a bad decision and followed it to its logical end. That turned out to be enough. The novel demonstrated that serious literature could look forward instead of backward, and that scientific imagination was not a novelty but a responsibility.

Takeaway: Frankenstein proved that the future asks better questions than the past, and that one young writer, armed with curiosity and very little supervision, can open a narrative frontier that still refuses to close.

1/5/1933 CONSTRUCTION OF THE GOLDEN GATE
A BOLD ENGINEERING GAMBLE RISES OVER A TREACHEROUS STRAIT

Work on the Golden Gate Bridge began on 5 January 1933, an undertaking so ambitious that skeptics predicted it would either bankrupt California or collapse into the Pacific at the first strong gust of wind. The Golden Gate Strait was notorious: violent tides, unpredictable fog, and winds capable of rattling steel. Building a suspension bridge across it seemed reckless—unless it succeeded. Then it would become a monument to American engineering, New Deal optimism, and the enduring human impulse to build something impressive simply because the ocean is in the way.

San Francisco Bay

Joseph Strauss, the project's chief engineer, championed the bridge with relentless determination. His early designs were clunky hybrids—part suspension, part cantilever—that horrified architects. After enough protest, Strauss accepted a redesigned, graceful suspension structure contributed by Charles Ellis and Leon Moisseiff. Their work transformed the bridge from functional curiosity into an iconic silhouette before construction even started.

Financing the project proved equally daunting. The Great Depression strangled investment, and federal assistance wavered. Local citizens, desperate for jobs and hopeful for economic revival, approved bond measures secured against future tolls. Once funding stabilized, the challenge shifted to logistics. Workers dangled from cables hundreds of feet above water, navigating wind, fog, and the constant threat of fatal falls. Strauss instituted strict safety measures, including hard hats and a massive safety net that saved nineteen men—later nicknamed the "halfway to hell club."

Construction advanced faster than expected. Towers rose like red monoliths through the mist, cables thickened into shimmering arcs, and the roadway extended inch by inch toward completion. By 1937 the bridge stood ready, a 1.7 mile span painted in International Orange—a color chosen not for beauty but for visibility in the endless fog. Beauty was incidental; the color became legendary.

When the bridge opened, crowds flooded across it, celebrating not just a structure but a symbolic triumph. The Golden Gate Bridge represented a recovery of confidence during the Depression, a declaration that even in hard times the nation could build something daring, elegant, and enduring.

Takeaway: The Golden Gate Bridge showed that great engineering projects begin with disbelief, endure through risk, and finish as symbols for people who need reminders that ambition survives uncertainty.

1/7/1610 GALILEO DISCOVERS JUPITER'S MOONS
FOUR SATELLITES OVERTURN THE UNIVERSE FROM A BACKYARD TELESCOPE

Galileo Galilei aimed his improved telescope at Jupiter on 7 January 1610 and discovered something that permanently shifted humanity's understanding of the cosmos. He observed what appeared to be three bright stars near the planet. Over subsequent nights, he noticed they moved—not randomly, but around Jupiter. A fourth appeared soon after. These were the moons Io, Europa, Ganymede, and Callisto. The discovery undermined centuries of geocentric doctrine and offered proof that not everything revolved around Earth.

The prevailing view, endorsed by Aristotle and defended by the Church, insisted Earth sat immobile at the universe's center. Galileo's observations contradicted this neatly arranged system. If moons orbited Jupiter, then celestial bodies could revolve around something other than Earth. It was a small detail with enormous

Portrait of scientist Galileo Galilei

implications, opening the door for the Copernican model and raising uncomfortable questions about human importance in the cosmic order.

Galileo acted like a scientist and a showman. He published his findings quickly in "Sidereus Nuncius" (The Starry

Messenger), a work that blended precision with provocation. Scholars gasped. Clergy frowned. Astronomers scrambled to replicate or refute his results. For those who looked through comparable telescopes, the evidence was obvious. Jupiter had moons. The heavens were not perfect crystalline spheres. The universe was more dynamic, more complex, and less flattering to human ego than previously imagined.

The Church, initially cautious, grew hostile as Galileo pushed his interpretations too publicly. His discoveries contributed to the tensions that later led to his trial. Yet the damage to the geocentric worldview was irreversible. Observational science had confronted inherited doctrine and proved more reliable.

Galileo's four moons remain among the most studied bodies in the solar system. Europa's icy ocean, Io's volcanic activity, Ganymede's magnetic field—they now fuel scientific ambition he could not have imagined. But the real revolution occurred in 1610, when a man with a telescope dismantled an entire cosmology in a single winter night.

Takeaway: Galileo's discovery proved that the universe does not bend to human assumptions, and that a simple observation can overturn centuries of confident error.

1/10/1776 COMMON SENSE PUBLISHED

A PAMPHLET TURNS FRUSTRATION INTO REVOLUTION

On 10 January 1776, Common Sense was published in Philadelphia, and within weeks it did something no colonial newspaper or polite petition had managed to do. It made independence sound obvious. Written by Thomas Paine, the pamphlet dismantled the idea of monarchy, ridiculed hereditary rule, and argued that separation from Britain was not radical but overdue.

Paine did not write for elites. He wrote for tradesmen, farmers, laborers, and anyone tired of pretending loyalty to a distant king made sense. His language was direct, confrontational, and intentionally accessible. He framed monarchy as absurd, kings as unnecessary, and reconciliation as fantasy. Britain was not a misunderstood parent. It was an obstacle.

Thomas Paine by Peter Kramer, 1851

The timing mattered. Colonial resentment had been simmering for years, but many still hoped for compromise. Paine eliminated that middle ground. He argued that continued submission was not prudence but cowardice, and that delay only strengthened tyranny. Independence, he insisted, was not just desirable but inevitable. The pamphlet spread rapidly, selling tens of thousands of copies in a population barely accustomed to mass political reading.

Colonial leaders noticed immediately. Some welcomed the clarity. Others worried Paine had gone too far, too fast, and too publicly. He had. And that was the point. By stripping away legal caution and diplomatic language, Common Sense shifted the conversation from whether independence was possible to why it had not already happened.

Within six months, the Continental Congress adopted language that would have sounded reckless before January. The Declaration of Independence followed in July. Paine did not draft it, but he prepared the audience. The revolution did not begin with gunfire alone. It required permission to think differently, and Paine handed it out freely.

The pamphlet's influence outlasted the war. It established a model for political persuasion that favored clarity over deference and moral argument over tradition. It proved that ideas, when written plainly enough, could outrun armies and embarrass empires.

Takeaway: Common Sense proved that revolutions do not begin when leaders agree, but when ordinary people stop accepting explanations that no longer survive inspection.

1/11/1935 Earhart Flies Solo from Hawaii to California

A Pilot Outflies Danger, Doubt, and the Pacific's Worst Intentions

Amelia Earhart completed her solo flight from Honolulu to Oakland on 11 January 1935, becoming the first person—man or woman—to fly alone across that treacherous stretch of the Pacific. The route was unforgiving. Winds were unstable, weather unpredictable, and the margin for error nonexistent. Several pilots attempting the same flight had died. Earhart's success transformed her from aviation icon to global legend.

She took off in a Lockheed Vega, navigating nearly 2,400 miles over open ocean with no safe place to land and no forgiveness for mechanical failure. Radio contact was limited. This being a night flight increased the challenge, all the more. Earhart relied on skill, intuition, and the stubborn belief that limits existed only to be negotiated with. Hours passed in darkness and turbulence until the California coast finally emerged through the haze.

The landing in Oakland triggered pandemonium. Crowds flooded the runway. Reporters scrambled for quotes. Headlines declared her the "Queen of the Air." Yet Earhart downplayed the achievement, calling the flight "mostly routine," a description only someone with an iron temperament could deliver after surviving a journey that had claimed others.

Her flight carried symbolic weight beyond aviation. It challenged assumptions about gender, capability, and courage. Earhart had already crossed the Atlantic, won races, and set records, but the Hawaii to California flight elevated her into myth. She demonstrated that risk did not discriminate and neither did mastery.

The accomplishment intensified public fascination, fueling her advocacy for women in aviation and her push for broader opportunities in professional fields. Earhart's influence extended beyond cockpits; she provided a model of independence that resonated far outside the world of flight.

Two years later, she attempted her round-the-world journey and vanished over the Pacific, deepening the legend she had spent her career inadvertently constructing. But her 1935 triumph remains a milestone, not because she survived danger, but because she chose to confront it with precision and confidence.

Takeaway: Earhart's flight proved that boundaries exist mostly in the imagination, and that courage becomes contagious when someone demonstrates what the impossible actually looks like.

1/12/1910 FIRST RADIO BROADCAST OF A SPORTING EVENT
A SINGLE MICROPHONE DOES NOT INVENT SPORTS RADIO, BUT IT STARTS ASKING THE RIGHT QUESTIONS

Lee De Forest American inventor

On 12 January 1910, something new crackled through the air. Lee De Forest, an inventor with a talent for audacity, transmitted the voice of Enrico Caruso from the Metropolitan Opera House using experimental radio equipment. This was not a sporting event, and it was not mass broadcasting. It was a proof of concept. Sound could travel without wires. That was enough to make people uneasy and curious at the same time.

The audience was small, mostly engineers, hobbyists, and anyone with the patience to build or tune a receiver. There were no sponsors, no schedules, and no guarantee that anything would be heard clearly. Static competed with music. Interference won often. Still, the implication was obvious. If a voice could travel, so could excitement.

Sports would eventually provide the perfect test case. Boxing matches, baseball games, and football contests offered motion, suspense, and stakes. But in 1910, the technology was not ready. Microphones were crude. Amplification was weak. Reliable live narration had not yet been invented as a skill. Early experiments were closer to demonstrations than broadcasts.

The real shift came later. After World War I, radio infrastructure improved. Receivers entered homes. Stations began regular programming. By the early 1920s, live sports broadcasts reached large audiences, most famously with boxing matches like Jack Dempsey versus Georges Carpentier, carried by stations such as KDKA. That was when sports radio stopped being an experiment and became a habit.

Once scale arrived, consequences followed quickly. Teams gained distant fans. Athletes became voices as well as faces. Newspapers adapted instead of collapsing. Stadiums filled rather than emptied. Radio did not replace live sports, it advertised them. Business followed attention, as it always does.

Radio ultimately changed how events were shared. A moment no longer belonged only to those present. A fight, a play, or a final score could ripple outward in real time, stitching together listeners who would never meet.

The first transmissions were uneven, fragile, and frequently disappointing. That was the point. They proved the idea before the infrastructure existed to support it. Everything that followed, the commentary, the commerce, the cultural obsession, grew from those early signals that barely survived the noise.

Takeaway: Radio did not instantly turn sports into mass entertainment. It learned how to listen first. Once it did, the crowd followed.

1/15/1967 First Super Bowl Held
A merger game becomes the nucleus of America's biggest sporting spectacle

The first Super Bowl was played on 15 January 1967, though it wasn't yet called the Super Bowl. Officially titled the AFL-NFL World Championship Game, it pitted the Green Bay Packers against the Kansas City Chiefs in Los Angeles. Football was popular, but it had not yet captured the national scale that baseball enjoyed. This game, born from a merger agreement between rival leagues, became the seed of a cultural institution.

The stadium was far from full. Tickets were affordable yet still unsold. The halftime show featured marching bands rather than pop stars. But the stakes mattered. The NFL, older and more established, needed to assert dominance. The AFL wanted legitimacy. Vince Lombardi's Packers delivered a methodical win—35 to 10—that reinforced the NFL's reputation. The Chiefs played well early, but Green Bay's discipline and execution overwhelmed them.

What the first game lacked in spectacle, it made up for in potential. Television executives saw the future. Advertisers recognized a captive audience. Within a few years, the rebranded Super Bowl transformed into a national ritual—equal parts sport, entertainment, and economic machine. Today's extravaganza began with a half empty stadium, modest production values, and an uncertain public.

Takeaway: The first Super Bowl proved that even the largest cultural events start quietly, becoming institutions only when audiences decide the spectacle belongs to them.

1/18/1919 BENTLEY MOTORS FOUNDED
A COMPANY BUILT ON SPEED, ENGINEERING OBSESSION, AND UNAPOLOGETIC EXCESS

Bentley Motors was founded on 18 January 1919 by Walter Owen Bentley, an engineer convinced that cars could be both fast and durable—a combination few manufacturers of the era achieved. Bentley had served in World War I designing aircraft engines renowned for power and reliability. After the war, he turned his attention to automobiles, believing he could build machines that embodied mechanical precision without sacrificing performance.

Bentley dashboard clock bearing the winged "B" and "EST. 1919," a direct reference to the company's founding by W.O. Bentley and its early emphasis on precision engineering and mechanical reliability.

Bentley's first cars were hand-built creations that prioritized engine strength and handling over cosmetic flair. The company quickly earned a reputation for producing vehicles capable of enduring long-distance racing without mechanical collapse. This toughness attracted a group of wealthy, thrill-seeking British drivers later nicknamed the "Bentley Boys." They piloted the cars at Le Mans, achieving repeated victories in the 1920s. These wins established Bentley as a brand associated with speed, prestige, and engineering seriousness.

But racing success did not guarantee business success. Bentley's commitment to craftsmanship produced beautiful machines at ruinous cost. The company struggled financially even as its cars dominated endurance competitions. By 1931, economic pressure forced Bentley into receivership. Rolls-Royce purchased the company, preserving the brand while redirecting it toward luxury.

Despite the corporate takeover, Bentley retained its identity. It became a symbol of British motoring heritage, blending engineering rigor with refined excess. Postwar Bentleys offered speed with comfort, earning a clientele that preferred quiet power over flamboyant display. The brand evolved, but the engineering ethos remained: performance mattered, and reliability was non-negotiable.

In the modern era, Bentley continues to produce high-end vehicles that merge craftsmanship with technology, preserving the legacy Walter Bentley began in a modest London workshop. The company's survival through wartime, economic collapse, and corporate reorganization speaks to the enduring appeal of machines built with purpose rather than compromise.

Takeaway: Bentley's founding proved that engineering vision can outlast financial turbulence, and that excellence becomes identity when performance refuses to bend to cost.

1/24/1984 APPLE MACINTOSH INTRODUCED
A COMPUTER WITH A MOUSE AND A PERSONALITY RESHAPES AN INDUSTRY THAT PREFERRED BEIGE BOXES AND COMMAND LINES

Apple introduced the Macintosh on 24 January 1984 with a Super Bowl advertisement directed by Ridley Scott that promised to liberate humanity from conformity, followed by a computer that crashed frequently and could barely run useful software. The gap between marketing vision and product reality was enormous, yet somehow the Macintosh succeeded anyway—not immediately, but eventually, and not because it worked flawlessly but because it convinced people that computers could be tools for humans rather than puzzles for engineers.

The Macintosh was not the first computer with a graphical user interface. That distinction belonged to Xerox PARC, whose Alto workstation featured windows, icons, and a mouse in the 1970s. Xerox, a company that specialized in photocopiers and institutional inertia, failed to commercialize its own breakthrough. Steve Jobs visited PARC in 1979, saw the future, and decided Apple would build it instead. He was not stealing so much as rescuing good ideas from a company that could not recognize their value.

Apple's first attempt at a consumer-friendly GUI computer was the Lisa, released in 1983 at $10,000—a price point that ensured only corporations with experimental budgets and masochistic IT departments would consider it. The Lisa was technically impressive and commercially doomed. The Macintosh learned from that failure. It would be smaller, cheaper, and simpler. It would cost $2,495, still expensive but within reach of professionals, educators, and enthusiasts willing to mortgage their future for a beige box that smiled at them during startup.

Jobs unveiled the Macintosh at Apple's annual shareholder meeting with a performance that became legend. He pulled the computer from a bag, let it introduce itself with synthesized speech, and demonstrated a graphical interface that required no programming knowledge. The crowd erupted. Reporters scrambled. The mythology began immediately. But mythology and market success are not the same thing.

The original Macintosh shipped with 128 kilobytes of RAM—barely enough memory to hold a decent paragraph, let alone serious applications. It had no hard drive, relying on floppy disks that required constant swapping. It lacked a cooling fan, which kept it quiet but prone to overheating. The software library was thin. Businesses, already committed to IBM PCs running DOS, saw no reason to switch. The Macintosh was elegant, intuitive, and underpowered. Sales disappointed. Within months, inventory piled up. Jobs, never one for introspection when blame could be externalized, pushed harder on marketing while engineers scrambled to make the hardware functional.

What saved the Macintosh was not immediate commercial triumph but two developments that arrived later. First, desktop publishing. In 1985, the combination of the LaserWriter printer, Aldus PageMaker software, and the Mac's graphical interface created an entirely new industry. Suddenly, small businesses, design studios, and independent publishers could produce professional-quality documents without typesetting equipment or print shops. The Mac found its niche, and that niche turned into a market. Second, the Macintosh II in 1987—the computer the original Macintosh should have been— capable, expandable, and reliable enough for actual work. Sales climbed. The platform stabilized. Apple, despite Jobs' departure in 1985, kept refining the product line.

The Macintosh's true legacy was not technical superiority but conceptual shift. It demonstrated that computers did not need to be intimidating. The graphical interface—windows, icons, menus, pointers—became the standard. Microsoft copied it with Windows. The entire industry followed. By the 1990s, command-line interfaces were relics, and every operating system looked like a descendant of the ideas Xerox invented and Apple popularized.

The mythology around the Macintosh often credits Jobs alone, as if vision and presentation were equivalent to engineering. The reality involved hundreds of people: engineers who solved impossible problems, designers who made the interface elegant, and Xerox researchers who built the foundation. Jobs deserves credit for recognizing potential and forcing execution, but the Macintosh was a collective achievement dressed in a singular narrative because singular narratives sell better than committees.

The 1984 Super Bowl ad promised liberation. What the Macintosh actually delivered was accessibility. It did not free humanity from conformity—people still conformed, just with better fonts. But it lowered the barrier to computing, made technology approachable, and proved that interfaces mattered as much as processing power. The computer was no longer a tool exclusively for specialists. It became a tool for anyone willing to learn a few clicks.

Takeaway: The Macintosh proved that revolutionary products rarely work well at launch, but if the idea is sound and the marketing loud enough, the world will wait for the second version that actually functions.

1/25/1924 FIRST WINTER OLYMPICS OPEN IN CHAMONIX

WINTER SPORTS GAIN THEIR OWN GLOBAL ARENA

The first Winter Olympics began on 24 January 1924 in Chamonix, France, establishing a formal international competition dedicated to cold weather sports. Prior Olympic Games included occasional winter events, but the growing popularity of skiing, skating, and other icy athletics demanded a dedicated platform. The International Olympic Committee approved the idea, and athletes from sixteen nations converged on the alpine resort town.

Events included figure skating, hockey, bobsleigh, speed skating, and Nordic skiing. The atmosphere blended athletic ambition with improvisation. Facilities were functional rather than luxurious, and weather conditions frequently dictated schedules. Still, the competition captured global attention. Norway dominated the medal table, proving that countries with long winters held inherent strategic advantages.

The Winter Games legitimized winter sports as world class competitions, fostering international rivalries and popularizing disciplines that previously lacked global stages. Over time, the Winter Olympics expanded to include snowboarding, freestyle skiing, and other events that redefined athletic boundaries.

Chamonix's legacy endures not because the games were flawless but because they established a tradition. The inaugural event demonstrated that winter sports could attract spectators, inspire national pride, and sustain global interest.

Takeaway: The first Winter Olympics proved that athletic greatness is not limited by season, and that even a mountain town can launch an international tradition.

1/27/1967 APOLLO 1 TRAGEDY
PROGRESS MEETS FIRE IN A SEALED CAPSULE ON THE LAUNCHPAD

On 27 January 1967, astronauts Gus Grissom, Ed White, and Roger Chaffee died during a pre-launch test for Apollo 1 when a cockpit fire swept through their command module. The test was routine, conducted in a sealed cabin pressurized with pure oxygen. An electrical spark likely ignited flammable materials inside. Within seconds, the astronauts were overwhelmed; the hatch, designed to open inward, trapped them.

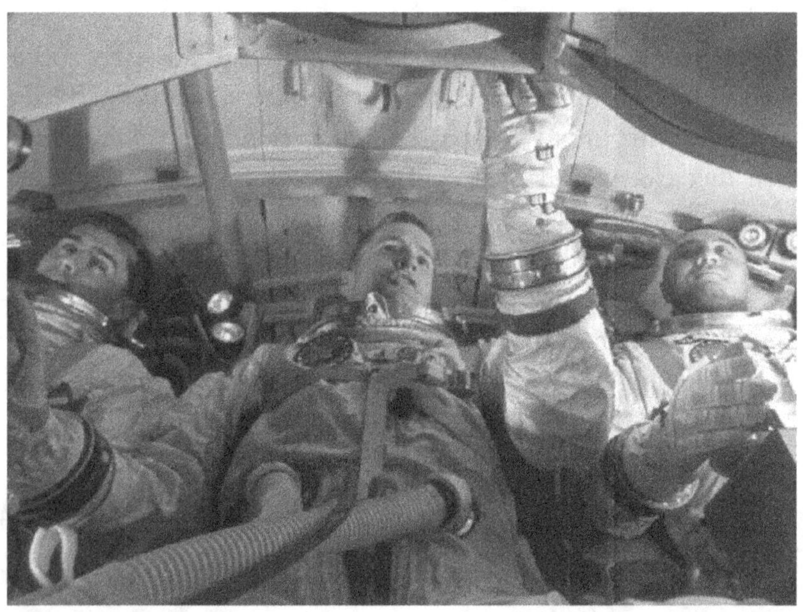

Astronauts for the first Apollo Mission (L-R) Roger B. Chaffee, Edward H. White and Virgil I. Grissom practice for the mission in the Apollo Mission Simulator.

The tragedy shocked NASA. The space race had emphasized speed over caution, driven by Cold War competition with the Soviet Union. Apollo 1 exposed the cost of that urgency. The program paused as investigators cataloged design flaws: wiring issues, combustible materials, and inadequate emergency procedures. Public confidence wavered. Critics questioned whether the moon landing goal justified the risks.

NASA responded with comprehensive redesigns. Engineers replaced flammable materials, reworked wiring systems, improved ventilation, and redesigned the hatch to open outward rapidly. The tragedy transformed Apollo into one of history's most intensively scrutinized engineering projects. The lessons carved into the program became essential to its later success.

Grissom, White, and Chaffee were honored as pioneers who paid the ultimate price in humanity's push toward space. Their deaths were not in vain; safety improvements implemented afterward enabled Apollo 11's triumph in 1969.

Apollo 1 remains a reminder that exploration demands precision, humility, and accountability. NASA's willingness to confront its failures ensured the program survived and succeeded.

Takeaway: Apollo 1 proved that ambition without safety becomes catastrophe, and that progress often requires rebuilding from the wreckage of its own mistakes.

1/28/1986 SPACE SHUTTLE CHALLENGER DISASTER
A PREVENTABLE FAILURE DESTROYS A CREW AND FORCES NASA BACK TO FUNDAMENTALS

The Space Shuttle Challenger exploded on 28 January 1986, seventy three seconds after liftoff, killing all seven crew members, including teacher Christa McAuliffe. Millions watched live. The disaster was not caused by mystery but by negligence: the failure of O-ring seals on a solid rocket booster. Engineers had warned that freezing temperatures compromised the rubber seals' integrity. NASA management dismissed those warnings under political pressure and scheduling demands.

The Rogers Commission investigation revealed a culture where concerns were softened, risks minimized, and technical objections treated as obstacles rather than safeguards. The Challenger disaster became a case study in institutional failure: groupthink overriding engineering judgment.

Public confidence collapsed. NASA grounded the shuttle fleet for years. Reforms strengthened oversight, redesigned booster joints, and altered launch decision protocols. The tragedy reshaped NASA's culture, reinforcing that spaceflight requires rigid safety discipline, not optimism.

Challenger's crew—McAuliffe, Scobee, Smith, Resnik, Onizuka, Jarvis, and McNair—became symbols of sacrifice in pursuit of exploration. Their loss forced the agency to choose between humility and hubris. NASA chose humility, and the shuttle program continued—but changed.

Takeaway: Challenger proved that failure often begins long before catastrophe, and that ignoring expert warnings turns risk into inevitability.

1/31/1958 EXPLORER 1 LAUNCHED
AMERICA ENTERS THE SPACE RACE UNDER PRESSURE AND WITH PURPOSE

Launch at Complex 26A, Cape Canaveral Air Force Station

Explorer 1 launched on 31 January 1958, becoming the first successful U.S. satellite and the country's direct answer to the Soviet Union's Sputnik shock. The psychological impact of Sputnik had been immediate and severe. It exposed American vulnerability, punctured assumptions of technological dominance, and generated a political climate where delay looked like weakness. Rocket malfunctions and humiliating test failures only intensified the urgency. By the time Explorer 1 reached the launch pad, success was not a luxury; it was a requirement for national credibility.

Explorer 1 was modest in size but ambitious in purpose. Lightweight, streamlined, and engineered with remarkable efficiency for its era, it carried scientific instruments rather than symbolic payloads. Physicist James Van Allen designed the onboard cosmic ray detector, a device intended to measure radiation levels in orbit. What it found exceeded expectations. The data revealed the presence of intense radiation zones encircling Earth, later named the Van Allen belts. This discovery reshaped scientific understanding of Earth's magnetosphere and showed that satellites could produce breakthroughs rather than mere propaganda victories.

The spacecraft's triumph did more than salvage national pride. It marked a structural turning point in American space efforts. Explorer 1 bridged the gap between scattered military rocket experiments and the more disciplined, coordinated program that would soon become NASA. It signaled that space exploration required long term investment, scientific rigor, and organizational unity rather than reactive competition alone. In its wake, the United States began developing the infrastructure, institutions, and strategic vision that ultimately carried astronauts to the Moon.

Takeaway: Explorer 1 proved that urgency can trigger innovation, but lasting advantage comes from science, structure, and the determination to build beyond crisis.

CLOSING REFLECTION

This chapter shows that knowledge does not advance by agreement or tradition, but by pressure. Reality applies force until explanations fracture, and once they do, replacement is unavoidable. Observation dismantles belief, engineering solidifies the outcome, and society adapts after the fact. The sequence is consistent across centuries. First comes evidence. Then comes construction. Then comes a world that behaves differently than it did before.

What begins as a challenge to understanding rarely stays contained. A corrected calendar restructures civic life. A telescope rearranges humanity's place in the universe. A bridge redraws geography. A broadcast collapses distance. A safety failure rewrites institutional behavior. Once knowledge is embedded into systems, it stops being optional. It becomes environment. People do not debate it, they live inside it.

Progress, then, is not a promise of improvement. It is a record of replacement. Old frameworks are discarded because they no longer function, not because they offend. New ones persist because they work, even when they introduce new risks and consequences. Science exposes what is wrong. Technology makes the correction unavoidable. Together, they ensure that the world moves forward whether comfort keeps pace or not.

CHAPTER 5

CONQUEST, MIGRATION, & TRANSFORMATION

WORLDS REMADE BY MOVEMENT AND POWER

Conquest, migration, exploration, and cultural transformation do not unfold as separate forces. They collide, overlap, and remake entire worlds whether anyone intends it or not. This chapter traces the movements of people and power across oceans and continents, revealing how quickly a landscape, a culture, or an idea can be altered once outsiders arrive or insiders are forced to move. Ellis Island compressed the immigrant experience into a single, anxious threshold that reshaped the United States through sheer volume. Australia's founding exposed how a penal colony could grow into a nation while inflicting irreversible damage on the people who were there first. Cook's voyages—whether pushing through Antarctic ice or stumbling upon Hawaiian shores—replaced fantasy with fact and isolation with contact, showing that exploration changes understanding even when it finds nothing of value, and destroys stability even when it claims to bring progress. The relentless tides of migration, conquest, and exploration did not simply populate maps. They reordered societies, redistributed power, and forced cultures into contact that produced reinvention, erasure, conflict, and endurance in unequal measure.

The battles included here—Princeton's desperate gambit and the Gulf War's overwhelming technological superiority—demonstrate that conquest comes in many forms: the scrappy survival of an underdog revolution and the precise devastation of modern military dominance. Henry VIII's institutional seizure of the Church of England proves that conquest need not involve armies when legislative authority can seize an entire civilization's spiritual infrastructure. The Wilhelm Gustloff's sinking reveals how war transforms migration into catastrophe, and how history remembers tragedy selectively based on who was fleeing and why.

Each event shows the same underlying truth: the world does not absorb change gradually. It fractures under pressure, reorganizes around new realities, and forces adaptation on everyone caught in the transformation. Immigrants process through Ellis Island not because America welcomes them warmly but because the nation needs their labor and demands their compliance. Gold seekers flood California not because of careful planning but because a few flakes of metal trigger a human avalanche that remakes an entire territory. The First Fleet anchors at Sydney Cove not to build paradise but to dump convicts, accidentally founding a nation while destroying another. Movement—whether driven by desperation, ambition, military force, or bureaucratic processing—never leaves the world intact.

Life Lesson: The world transforms whenever people move, explore, or impose themselves on new ground, and those shifts rarely unfold cleanly, fairly, or as their architects imagined.

1/1/1892 ELLIS ISLAND OPENS TO IMMIGRANTS
A BUREAUCRATIC GATEWAY BECOMES THE FIRST AMERICAN ADDRESS FOR MILLIONS

Ellis Island opened on 1 January 1892 as the United States' new federal immigration station, a facility built to replace the patchwork of state run systems that could no longer handle the volume of arrivals. The nation was in the middle of an industrial growth spurt. Cities expanded, factories multiplied, and steamship companies delivered human cargo by the thousands. The old methods of processing newcomers collapsed under the weight of the crowds. Washington stepped in, took control, and planted its flag on a small island in New York Harbor that would become the threshold of the American promise and the American inspection line.

The first arrival was Annie Moore, a fifteen year old Irish girl stepping into a facility that could handle five thousand people a day if the staff worked fast enough. They usually did. Inspectors operated with an efficiency that resembled a medical assembly line. Newcomers answered a battery of questions, endured a cursory physical exam, and attempted to remain calm while officials watched for signs of disease, disorientation, or anything that might suggest the government would be inheriting another problem.

For many, Ellis Island represented hope. For others, it represented anxiety. The Great Hall echoed with dozens of languages, suitcases thumped across floors, and families held tightly to one another in case the next question determined whether they stayed together or were split across borders. Most passed through without difficulty. A minority faced quarantine, further questioning, or rejection. The island became both a gate and a sieve, filtering dreams according to rules that could seem arbitrary even when officials insisted they were objective.

Over the next six decades, more than twelve million immigrants passed through the island. They arrived from Italy, Russia, Germany, Scandinavia, the Balkans, and beyond, each wave reshaping American demographics, labor markets, and cultural identity. Politicians argued about whether the nation was absorbing too many or too few. Newspapers warned of being overrun by unfamiliar languages, beliefs, and customs. The rhetoric never stopped, proving that debates over immigration were not a modern invention but a chronic American condition.

Ellis Island handled its work with escalating efficiency, expanding facilities, and adjusting protocols as federal laws shifted. Literacy tests were imposed; quotas followed. The island adapted to each new demand, transforming from an open gateway into a more restricted checkpoint as national mood hardened. By the mid twentieth century, the center's role faded. Air travel bypassed New York Harbor. Immigration laws changed. The station closed in 1954, leaving behind a monumental archive of names, faces, and first encounters.

The island eventually reopened as a museum, its halls preserved as a record of the millions who had walked through them, carrying expectations, fear, and whatever belongings had survived the voyage. Ellis Island became a symbol of national identity, not because it made the process gentle, but because it exposed the blunt mechanics of becoming American. It was rarely fair, rarely comfortable, but it was the gateway through which much of the modern nation arrived.

Takeaway: Ellis Island proved that the American dream begins with paperwork, scrutiny, and endurance, and that a nation of immigrants remembers its origins best when it remembers the gate that judged them.

1/3/1777 BATTLE OF PRINCETON
WASHINGTON SALVAGES A COLLAPSING REVOLUTION WITH A NIGHT MARCH, TACTICAL DECEPTION, AND THE STUBBORNNESS TO KEEP FIGHTING WHEN RETREAT LOOKED SMARTER

The Battle of Princeton on 3 January 1777 was not the largest engagement of the Revolutionary War, nor the most strategically significant. But it arrived at a moment when the Continental Army was disintegrating through desertion, expired enlistments, and the accumulated demoralization of six months of defeats. Washington's surprise attack on British forces at Princeton, following his Christmas night crossing of the Delaware and victory at Trenton, proved that the rebellion was not finished—just desperate, underfunded, and learning to turn desperation into tactical advantage. The battle transformed the war's momentum not because it crippled British military capacity but because it convinced enough people that independence was still possible, which turned out to be the only victory that mattered at that moment.

By late 1776, the Revolutionary War looked like a failed experiment approaching its conclusion. Washington had been chased out of New York, across New Jersey, and into Pennsylvania with an army that shrank daily. Enlistments expired at year's end. Soldiers went home. Supplies vanished. Morale collapsed. British General William Howe controlled New York and most of New Jersey, settling into winter quarters while assuming the rebellion would dissolve on its own by spring. He was not wrong to assume it. Washington commanded fewer than 5,000 effective troops, many shoeless, most exhausted, all aware that continuing the fight meant probable death with diminishing prospects of success.

Washington needed a victory to prevent total collapse. The attack on Trenton on 26 December delivered that victory—barely. His troops crossed the ice-choked Delaware in a winter storm, surprised the Hessian garrison, and captured nearly a thousand prisoners while suffering minimal casualties. It was brilliant, desperate, and temporary. British reinforcements under General Cornwallis marched south to crush Washington's small force. By 2 January, Cornwallis had Washington pinned against the Delaware River near Trenton with a superior force preparing to attack at dawn. The revolution appeared cornered.

Washington held a council of war. Retreat meant abandoning New Jersey and admitting defeat. Fighting Cornwallis directly meant annihilation. Washington chose a third option: deception. He ordered campfires kept burning, sentries posted loudly, and work crews digging entrenchments to create the illusion that his army was preparing to defend. Then, in darkness, the Continental Army abandoned the position and marched northeast on a back road toward Princeton, leaving behind a skeleton force to maintain the illusion until dawn.

The night march was miserable—freezing temperatures, rutted roads, exhausted men hauling artillery through mud. But by sunrise, Washington's army had circled behind Cornwallis and approached Princeton, where a smaller British force remained. The British were not expecting an attack from that direction or at that hour. The fighting was chaotic and close-range, starting in fields near the town and escalating into brutal exchanges where neither side held a clear advantage.

Washington personally rallied troops during the battle, riding forward into musket range in a moment that became legendary and probably should have gotten him killed. His presence steadied wavering units. The British garrison, outnumbered and surprised, fought hard but eventually broke. American forces pursued them through Princeton, capturing supplies, weapons, and prisoners. The victory was tactically modest—a few hundred British casualties and the capture of a small garrison. Strategically, it was transformative.

Cornwallis, discovering at dawn that Washington had vanished, raced his troops north toward Princeton only to find he had been outmaneuvered. Washington, rather than pressing his luck, marched his exhausted army to Morristown in the hills of northern New Jersey, establishing winter quarters in a defensible position that Cornwallis declined to attack. The "Ten Crucial Days" campaign—from crossing the Delaware to the victory at Princeton—salvaged the Continental Army's existence and proved that British forces were not invincible.

The psychological impact exceeded the military gains. Trenton and Princeton revived the rebellion when it was dying. Enlistments increased. Militia turned out. State legislatures renewed support. European powers, especially France, reconsidered whether the Americans might actually win. The battles demonstrated that Washington, despite his repeated defeats in 1776, possessed the tactical imagination and personal courage to keep fighting when conventional logic suggested surrender. He transformed desperation into strategy and proved that a weaker force could survive through maneuver, surprise, and refusal to accept the opponent's assumptions about when the war was over.

The British response revealed their strategic limitations. Howe had spent 1776 winning battles and occupying cities while failing to destroy Washington's army—the only objective that mattered. After Princeton, the British abandoned most of New Jersey, consolidating around New York and conceding territory they had conquered months earlier. The revolution, which had appeared crushed in December, controlled the countryside again by February. Washington had not defeated the British Empire. He had proven it could be resisted indefinitely, which was enough.

The battles also exposed the war's grim realities. Soldiers froze, starved, and deserted. Victories required luck as much as skill. The revolution survived not because Americans were united or committed but because enough people, at critical moments, decided collapse was worse than continuing. Washington's army at Princeton was not the mythical force of patriotic legend. It was a collection of desperate men who kept fighting because their commander refused to quit and because going home meant admitting the entire struggle had been pointless.

Princeton transformed Washington's reputation from competent commander to indispensable leader. His ability to salvage victory from near-disaster, to outthink opponents with superior resources, and to keep a collapsing army functional through personal leadership became the foundation of his legend. The crossing of the Delaware, the surprise at Trenton, and the bold march to Princeton created the narrative that sustained the revolution through six more years of hardship, defeat, and incremental progress toward independence.

Takeaway: Princeton proved that wars are won not by the side that never loses but by the side that refuses to quit after losing, and that sometimes the most important victory is the one that convinces everyone the fight is still worth continuing.

1/15/1535 CHURCH OF ENGLAND ESTABLISHED
A KING NEEDS A DIVORCE, SO HE CONQUERS GOD'S LOCAL REPRESENTATIVE AND REWRITES THE RULES

Henry VIII declared himself Supreme Head of the Church of England on 15 January 1535, completing a divorce from Rome that had nothing to do with theology and everything to do with Catherine of Aragon's failure to produce a male heir. The Pope refused to annul Henry's marriage, so Henry decided the Pope's authority was optional and established his own church—one with more flexible policies on royal remarriage. What began as dynastic desperation became institutional conquest. Henry wanted a new wife. He got a Reformation and control of England's richest organization.

Hereford Cathedral one of the church's 43 cathedrals

The crisis had been building since 1527, when Henry sought an annulment from Catherine. She had given him a daughter, Mary, but no surviving sons. Henry needed the Pope's approval. Pope Clement VII, recently humiliated by Holy Roman Emperor Charles V—who happened to be Catherine's nephew— found saying no to Henry politically safer than saying yes. Henry waited six years for Rome's approval. It never came.

By 1533, Henry's patience expired along with Anne Boleyn's willingness to remain merely his mistress. Henry married Anne and tasked Thomas Cranmer, the newly appointed Archbishop of Canterbury, with declaring his first marriage invalid. Rome excommunicated him. Henry responded by severing England's ties to the Catholic Church entirely and declaring himself head of a new English church—identical to the old one, but with better marriage policies.

Parliament formalized the break through a series of acts that stripped Rome of authority, redirected church revenue to the crown, and made opposition to the king's supremacy an act of treason. The Act of Supremacy in 1534 declared Henry "the only supreme head on earth of the Church of England." It was conquest without armies—Henry seized an entire institution through legislative fiat, confiscated its wealth, and eliminated anyone who objected too loudly. Thomas More, the former Lord Chancellor, refused to accept Henry's supremacy and was beheaded. John Fisher, the Bishop of Rochester, joined him. Dissent became martyrdom quickly.

The religious transformation was less than transformative initially. Henry remained theologically conservative—he rejected Protestant reforms, kept the Latin Mass, maintained clerical celibacy, and affirmed transubstantiation. The Church of England under Henry looked Catholic in everything except its refusal to acknowledge the Pope. It was Catholicism with a new CEO, not a new product.

The immediate consequences were financial and brutal. Henry dissolved the monasteries between 1536 and 1541, seizing their lands, wealth, and assets. Monks and nuns were evicted. Religious houses that had stood for centuries were dismantled or repurposed. The crown's income tripled. The aristocracy, rewarded with monastic lands, became invested in preserving the Reformation because returning to Rome would mean surrendering their new estates. Henry's break with the Pope enriched the state and created a propertied class with financial incentives to resist Catholic restoration.

The institutional seizure was thorough. Henry controlled doctrine, appointed bishops, collected revenues, and determined policy. The church's administrative machinery—its courts, its lands, its educational institutions—all transferred to royal authority. What had been an international organization with divided loyalties became a national institution wholly subordinate to the crown. It was the most complete institutional takeover in English history, accomplished through paperwork rather than bloodshed, though blood followed soon enough for dissenters.

The transformation unleashed religious violence that lasted generations. Edward VI pushed the church toward Protestantism. Mary I tried to reverse it through persecution, earning the nickname "Bloody Mary." Elizabeth I finally stabilized the church through a via media—a middle way that blended Catholic structure with Protestant theology. The English Civil War in the 1640s partly stemmed from unresolved religious tensions Henry had unleashed.

Ironically, Henry never intended to create a lasting Protestant nation. He wanted a divorce, a son, and continued control. The son never materialized—not a legitimate male heir who survived him. Anne Boleyn gave him another daughter, Elizabeth, before Henry had her beheaded. His third wife, Jane Seymour, produced Edward, who died at fifteen. Henry's quest for dynastic security produced exactly the opposite: a succession crisis and religious instability that nearly tore England apart.

Yet the Church of England endured. It became a defining feature of English identity, a symbol of independence from continental powers, and a theological compromise that allowed coexistence between Catholic tradition and Protestant reform. What Henry created out of frustrated lust became an institution that outlasted empires.

Henry's supremacy over the Church was conquest of a different kind—not territorial but institutional. He seized control of the most powerful organization in England, redirected its loyalty from Rome to the crown, and transformed religious authority into royal prerogative. It was personal ambition scaled to national transformation, proof that reshaping civilization sometimes requires nothing more than a king who refuses to take no for an answer.

Takeaway: Henry VIII proved that divorce can be more revolutionary than theology, and that when a king decides to rewrite the rules for personal convenience, the consequences last far longer than the marriage that started it.

1/17/1991 GULF WAR BEGINS
A DICTATOR INVADES HIS NEIGHBOR, THE WORLD RESPONDS WITH OVERWHELMING FORCE, AND EVERYONE PRETENDS THE PROBLEM IS SOLVED

Operation Desert Storm began on 17 January 1991 when coalition aircraft struck targets across Iraq and Kuwait, launching a war that would be over in forty-two days and never actually end. Saddam Hussein had invaded Kuwait the previous August, annexing the tiny oil-rich nation and betting that the world would complain loudly but do nothing substantive. He miscalculated. The United States, freshly victorious in the Cold War and eager to demonstrate what a unipolar world looked like, assembled a coalition of thirty-five nations, secured United Nations approval, and prepared to remove Iraqi forces with a level of military precision that resembled a product demonstration.

The air campaign opened with cruise missiles, stealth bombers, and a technological superiority so overwhelming it looked almost unfair. Iraqi air defenses crumbled within hours. Command centers, communication networks, and infrastructure dissolved under guided munitions launched from distances Saddam's military could not comprehend, let alone counter. CNN broadcast the war live, turning combat into spectacle. Reporters narrated from hotel balconies in Baghdad while bombs lit the sky like fireworks. Viewers watched grainy green footage of missiles threading through windows and bridges collapsing in real time. It was the first war consumed as entertainment, complete with graphics packages and retired generals providing play-by-play analysis.

Saddam had assumed the international community would tolerate his conquest the way it had tolerated his previous aggressions. Iraq had fought an eight-year war with Iran that the West quietly supported because Iran was the larger concern.

Saddam believed Kuwait was a rogue province, carved out by colonial powers with no legitimate claim to independence. He also believed the United States, scarred by Vietnam, would avoid another Middle Eastern conflict. He was wrong on all counts.

President George H.W. Bush framed the war as a defense of international order, a line in the sand against naked aggression. The rhetoric was noble. The motivations were practical. Kuwait sat atop vast oil reserves. Saudi Arabia, even more critical to global energy markets, bordered Iraq and feared it was next. Allowing Saddam to control that much oil would destabilize the region and the global economy. The coalition formed not out of humanitarian concern but because conquest threatened profits and power structures too valuable to ignore.

The ground war, when it finally launched in late February, lasted one hundred hours. Coalition forces swept through Iraqi positions with such speed that retreating Iraqi troops fled Kuwait in chaotic convoys, which were then obliterated along the "Highway of Death" in scenes so one-sided they generated discomfort even among those who supported the war. Iraqi soldiers surrendered en masse, many starving, demoralized, and abandoned by commanders who had already fled. The Kuwaiti government was restored. Bush declared victory and halted the advance, choosing not to march on Baghdad or remove Saddam from power.

That decision, pragmatic at the time, ensured the conflict would never truly conclude. Saddam remained in control, humiliated but dangerous, suppressing uprisings with chemical weapons while the coalition imposed sanctions and no-fly zones. The Gulf War became a frozen conflict, a military victory without political resolution. Iraqi civilians suffered under economic sanctions that weakened the population far more than the leadership. Saddam rebuilt his military, defied weapons inspectors, and waited.

The war demonstrated American military dominance but also revealed the limits of overwhelming force. You can win battles decisively and still fail to achieve strategic objectives. The coalition's restraint in 1991—leaving Saddam in power to avoid chaos—set the stage for the 2003 invasion, which removed Saddam but proved chaos was arriving regardless. The Gulf War became the first chapter in a longer story of American entanglement in Iraq, a story that continues decades later with no clear conclusion.

Militarily, Desert Storm was a triumph. Technologically, it showcased precision warfare. Politically, it was incomplete. The war ended with parades, yellow ribbons, and declarations that the "Vietnam Syndrome" was finally over. American military confidence soared. But the broader Middle East did not stabilize. Regional tensions deepened. The war's lingering presence—sanctions, no-fly zones, ongoing military deployments—fueled resentment and radicalization that would manifest a decade later in ways the coalition never anticipated.

The Gulf War was sold as a clean victory, a demonstration that modern warfare could be swift, precise, and limited. It was all those things, and it solved nothing permanent. Saddam survived. Kuwait was liberated but never the same. Iraq's infrastructure was shattered. The coalition declared success and went home, leaving behind a region more fractured than before and a dictator with a grudge and two more decades to nurse it.

Takeaway: Operation Desert Storm proved that overwhelming military victory is easy when you have better technology, but winning a war decisively is meaningless if you don't know what comes next or lack the will to finish what you started.

1/17/1773 COOK CROSSES THE ANTARCTIC CIRCLE
EXPLORATION PUSHES SOUTH UNTIL THE MAP RUNS OUT

Captain James Cook crossed the Antarctic Circle on 17 January 1773, becoming the first recorded explorer to breach the boundary of Earth's southernmost waters. The expedition—cold, dangerous, and navigationally uncertain—pushed deeper into the planet's least understood region. European maps still imagined Antarctica as a theoretical "great southern continent," often drawn large because speculation required no cartographic restraint. Cook's journey confronted myth with experience.

The Ice Islands, Seen the 9th of Jan. 1773

Sailing aboard the Resolution, Cook battled fog, shifting ice, and temperatures that rendered ropes brittle and decks treacherous. The expedition's purpose was not to find land for colonization but to understand whether the massive continent imagined by geographers even existed. Cook's instruments froze. His men operated under constant threat of icebergs capable of splitting hulls open with no warning. The southern ocean offered none of the tropical charm associated with exploration; it presented monotony, cold, and danger.

When Cook crossed the Antarctic Circle, he entered a realm no European had confirmed. He found not a continent but fields of pack ice stretching to the horizon. Cook pressed onward until the frozen barrier made further progress impossible. He speculated that if a southern continent existed, it lay beyond the reach of wooden ships and human endurance. His conclusion shaped European understanding of the region for decades and deterred further attempts to penetrate the ice until technological improvements made polar exploration viable in the nineteenth century.

Cook's expedition charted new waters, collected scientific data, and underscored the limits of maritime exploration. The voyage reinforced his reputation as the most accomplished navigator of his era. Although he did not see Antarctica, he proved that the imagined southern landmass was not the warm, fertile continent earlier theorists had pictured. Cook's report replaced speculation with cold, literal reality.

The crossing marked the moment when exploration began transitioning from imperial ambition to scientific endeavor. Cook's observations influenced navigation, meteorology, and geography, aligning exploration with empirical method rather than imaginative projection.

Takeaway: Cook's crossing proved that exploration's greatest value lies not in confirming myths but in disproving them, and that some boundaries yield only to those willing to face landscapes that offer no reward except truth.

1/18/1778 CAPTAIN COOK ENCOUNTERS HAWAII
A NAVIGATIONAL SUCCESS THAT OPENED A PARADISE TO CONSEQUENCES IT DID NOT REQUEST

British explorer James Cook sighted the Hawaiian Islands in January 1778 during his third Pacific voyage. To European navigators, the encounter appeared routine, another successful charting of land previously unknown to their maps. To the people of Hawaii, it marked the beginning of sustained contact with a world that would permanently disrupt their society, economy, and sovereignty.

Cook named the islands the Sandwich Islands, a branding choice that managed to honor his patron while completely ignoring the civilization already living there. His journals described fertile land, skilled seafarers, and a society that appeared orderly, generous, and strategically located. For European powers, that combination read as opportunity. For Hawaiians, it marked the arrival of outsiders who would not leave quietly.

Initial contact was cautious but relatively peaceful. Trade followed. Curiosity flowed both ways. But Cook's reports did what exploration reports always did, they translated living cultures into resources, ports, and potential leverage. The islands sat astride key Pacific routes. Whalers, traders, missionaries, and imperial interests took note. Hawaii was no longer isolated. It was scheduled.

Cook returned to the islands later that year under less favorable conditions. Tensions rose, misunderstandings compounded, and cultural assumptions collided. In February 1779, Cook was killed during a confrontation at Kealakekua Bay, a moment that shattered the myth of European invulnerability and foreshadowed the instability contact would bring.

The long term consequences unfolded without haste. Disease reduced the native population catastrophically. Foreign influence reshaped governance. Economic integration favored outsiders. What began as a navigational footnote evolved into annexation, plantation economies, and the steady erosion of sovereignty.

Cook's journals, like so many exploration records, were accurate in detail and disastrous in implication. They did not invent imperial ambition, but they provided it with coordinates.

Takeaway: Cook's encounter with Hawaii proved that discovery is rarely mutual, and that when explorers write the first draft of history, the people being described usually pay the highest price later.

1/24/1848 GOLD DISCOVERED AT SUTTER'S MILL
A FEW FLAKES OF METAL TRIGGER ONE OF HISTORY'S MOST CHAOTIC MIGRATIONS

Gold was discovered at Sutter's Mill on 24 January 1848 when James Marshall spotted shiny flakes in the water of the American River in California. The discovery occurred at a sawmill owned by John Sutter, who hoped to keep it secret. Secrecy lasted minutes. News spread through whispers, newspapers, and rumors that multiplied faster than facts. By 1849, tens of thousands of fortune seekers—"forty-niners"—flooded into California from across the United States, Latin America, Europe, and Asia.

The Gold Rush transformed California instantly. Tent cities exploded into chaotic boomtowns. Merchants, miners, gamblers, and opportunists converged on the region. Supplies vanished as quickly as they arrived. Prices soared. Roads turned to sludge in winter and dust in summer. Crime surged. Fortune rarely favored miners; merchants selling tools, food, and clothing earned far more. Levi Strauss built an empire on durable pants while most miners dug only disappointment.

Native populations suffered catastrophic displacement, violence, and disease. Environmental destruction followed hydraulic mining, which tore mountainsides apart and filled rivers with debris. Yet the Gold Rush accelerated California's path to statehood, expanded American economic networks, and intensified the doctrine of Manifest Destiny.

For those who struck gold, the wealth could be transformative. But most found only exhaustion. The Gold Rush became a lesson in American ambition—boundless, chaotic, and indifferent to the human cost.

Takeaway: Sutter's Mill proved that a discovery measured in ounces can unleash consequences measured in nations.

1/26/1788 AUSTRALIA DAY: FIRST FLEET ARRIVES AT SYDNEY COVE

A PENAL COLONY BECOMES THE FOUNDATION OF A MODERN NATION

Australia Day commemorates 26 January 1788, when Captain Arthur Phillip and the First Fleet anchored at Sydney Cove to establish a British penal outpost in New South Wales. Britain, facing overcrowded prisons and social strain in the aftermath of the American Revolution, sought a new location to deposit convicts. The decision to settle Australia was driven less by grand strategy and more by desperation and convenience.

Raising the British flag at Sydney Cove, 1788—where Britain's prison overflow became a nation.

The fleet carried more than 1,300 people: marines, sailors, officers, and hundreds of convicts sentenced for crimes ranging from petty theft to violent offenses. Conditions aboard the ships were grim, but the real challenge awaited them on land.

The settlers faced an unfamiliar climate, scarce resources, and logistical chaos. Indigenous Australians, whose presence stretched back tens of thousands of years, confronted a sudden occupation that would trigger centuries of conflict, displacement, and cultural destruction.

Phillip established the camp with a blend of discipline and improvisation. Supplies ran low quickly. Tools broke. Crops failed. Convicts labored under harsh conditions, and the settlement's survival often depended on sheer perseverance. Yet the colony endured, eventually expanding through exploration, migration, and the forced labor of transported prisoners.

Australia Day remains contested. For many non-Indigenous Australians, it represents the beginning of national identity. For Indigenous communities, it marks invasion, dispossession, and the painful beginning of colonial domination. The tension reflects the complexity of the continent's history: achievement and atrocity intertwined.

The arrival at Sydney Cove began a transformation that would reshape the continent politically, economically, and demographically. What started as a penal colony grew into a federation of states and territories that became the Commonwealth of Australia in 1901. But the origin remains inseparable from its costs.

Takeaway: Australia Day proved that nations often begin in contradiction, celebrated by some and mourned by others, and that founding moments rarely carry a single meaning.

1/30/1945 WILHELM GUSTLOFF SINKING
THE DEADLIEST MARITIME DISASTER IN HISTORY GETS FORGOTTEN BECAUSE THE VICTIMS WERE ON THE WRONG SIDE

The Wilhelm Gustloff sank on 30 January 1945 in the frigid Baltic Sea after being torpedoed by a Soviet submarine, killing an estimated 9,000 people—six times more than the Titanic. It remains the deadliest maritime disaster in recorded history, yet most people have never heard of it. The reason is straightforward: the passengers were German civilians fleeing the advancing Red Army, and by 1945, global sympathy for German suffering had been exhausted by six years of war, genocide, and aggression that Germany had initiated. Tragedy does not pause for moral accounting, but memory does.

The ship had been designed as a cruise liner for the Nazi "Strength Through Joy" program, meant to provide vacations for loyal workers in a regime that specialized in packaging brutality as social benefits. By 1945, it had been repurposed as a refugee vessel, part of Operation Hannibal—the largest maritime evacuation in history, moving over two million Germans out of East Prussia as Soviet forces closed in. The Eastern Front had collapsed. The Red Army was advancing with well-earned fury, and German civilians in the path understood what Soviet occupation meant: retribution for the horrors Germany had inflicted on the Soviet Union.

The Gustloff was rated to carry fewer than 2,000 people. On its final voyage, it held somewhere between 9,000 and 10,600—no one is certain because record-keeping disintegrated along with the German state. The passengers were mostly women, children, and elderly, along with wounded soldiers and naval personnel. They crowded into every available space: cabins, corridors, drained swimming pools, anywhere that offered a chance of escape. The ship departed Gotenhafen (now Gdynia, Poland) in a desperate run toward safety that would last only a few hours.

Soviet submarine S-13, commanded by Captain Alexander Marinesko, spotted the Gustloff and fired three torpedoes. All three struck. The ship listed immediately, trapping thousands below deck in darkness as seawater flooded compartments. Lifeboats, inadequate even for the ship's designed capacity, were frozen to their davits or swamped by the panicking crowds. The Baltic in January is lethally cold—survival time in the water measured in minutes. Most passengers never reached lifeboats. They drowned inside the ship or died of hypothermia within moments of entering the sea.

The Gustloff sinking after being hit.

Rescue ships saved approximately 1,000 people. The remaining 9,000 perished in what remains the single deadliest sinking in maritime history. The event was chaos without heroism, tragedy without redemption. There were no orchestras playing as the ship went down, no orderly queues, no time for the myths that soften disaster. Just cold water, screaming, and mass death delivered efficiently by modern warfare.

Marinesko received a delayed Hero of the Soviet Union award, though his superiors initially hesitated because he had a reputation for drinking and insubordination. The attack was legal under the laws of war—the Gustloff was a military target carrying armed personnel, even if most passengers were civilians. International law offered no comfort to the dead. The sinking was strategic from a Soviet perspective: one more blow against a collapsing enemy. From the passengers' perspective, it was annihilation.

The tragedy is largely forgotten in the West, overshadowed by the Holocaust, Allied victories, and a postwar narrative that had little room for German civilian suffering. Germany itself was hesitant to emphasize the story, aware that mourning its own victims while the world cataloged German atrocities looked like deflection. The Gustloff became a footnote, a statistic too large to ignore but too uncomfortable to dwell on.

Yet the sinking exposes the mechanism of total war: civilians become targets because they exist on the wrong side of a conflict they did not necessarily choose. The passengers fleeing East Prussia were not Nazi officials or SS officers—they were people trying not to die, caught in the collapse of a regime they had lived under but not necessarily controlled. War's final stages are the cruelest because retreat amplifies suffering. The guilty and innocent flee together, and the pursuing army rarely distinguishes.

Operation Hannibal ultimately evacuated over two million people, making it one of history's most successful large-scale rescues despite losses like the Gustloff. But success is relative. Millions escaped Soviet occupation, yet thousands drowned, froze, or were killed in transit. The operation demonstrated that even in defeat, organized effort could save lives—and that saving lives in war requires accepting that many will be lost anyway.

The Wilhelm Gustloff sinking stands as a reminder that history's deadliest disasters are not always its most remembered, and that moral complexity does not pause during wartime. The victims were German, but they were also human. Their deaths were legal under the laws of war, but legality and tragedy are not opposites. The ship went down carrying people who had lived under an evil regime, but dying in freezing water does not require ideological purity to be horrific.

Takeaway: The Wilhelm Gustloff proved that the deadliest disasters are often the least remembered, and that history's sympathy depends not on the scale of suffering but on who was suffering and why.

CLOSING REFLECTION

Movement, whether driven by ambition, desperation, or conquest, never leaves the world intact. The events in this chapter show how quickly landscapes, cultures, and identities can be rewritten once new arrivals appear or old populations are pushed aside. Ellis Island turned migration into a national mechanism, reshaping the United States through sheer scale. Australia's founding revealed how empire builds a nation while dismantling another. Columbus's triumphant letter unleashed centuries of expansion that reshaped entire continents, while Cook's voyage stripped myth from geography and replaced it with cold reality. Even accidental discoveries, like the strike at Sutter's Mill, sent shockwaves that reordered economies and societies far beyond their point of origin. Each episode demonstrates that contact between peoples does not simply add new layers to the world; it alters the structure itself, often through upheaval that later generations inherit without remembering its cost.

SCAN THE QR CODE ABOVE FOR MORE BOOKS IN
THE NOMICAL HISTORY SERIES.

Sources & Further Reading

This book is written with humor, but the history is real. If you'd like to explore the events beyond my commentary, here are the main sources and references used:

Ascher, Abraham. *The Revolution of 1905: Russia in Disarray*. Stanford, CA: Stanford University Press, 1988.

Bainton, Roland H. *Here I Stand: A Life of Martin Luther*. Nashville: Abingdon-Cokesbury Press, 1950.

Bliss, Michael. *The Discovery of Insulin*. Chicago: University of Chicago Press, 1982.

Branch, Taylor. *Parting the Waters: America in the King Years, 1954–1963*. New York: Simon & Schuster, 1988.

Brands, H. W. *The Age of Gold: The California Gold Rush and the New American Dream*. New York: Doubleday, 2002.

Butler, Susan. *East to the Dawn: The Life of Amelia Earhart*. New York: Da Capo Press, 1997.

Cadbury, Deborah. *Space Race: The Epic Battle Between America and the Soviet Union for Dominion of Space*. New York: HarperCollins, 2006.

Carson, Clayborne, ed. *The Autobiography of Martin Luther King, Jr.* New York: Warner Books, 1998.

Dawidowicz, Lucy S. *The War Against the Jews, 1933–1945*. New York: Holt, Rinehart and Winston, 1975.

DeVries, Kelly. *Joan of Arc: A Military Leader*. Stroud: Sutton Publishing, 1999.

Doyle, William. *The Oxford History of the French Revolution*. Oxford: Oxford University Press, 1989.

Dubois, Laurent. *Avengers of the New World: The Story of the Haitian Revolution*. Cambridge, MA: Harvard University Press, 2004.

Etcheson, Nicole. *Bleeding Kansas: Contested Liberty in the Civil War Era*. Lawrence: University Press of Kansas, 2004.

Figes, Orlando. *A People's Tragedy: The Russian Revolution, 1891–1924*. New York: Viking, 1996.

Foner, Eric. *The Fiery Trial: Abraham Lincoln and American Slavery*. New York: W. W. Norton, 2010.

Fraser, Antonia. *The Six Wives of Henry VIII*. New York: Knopf, 1992.

French, Patrick. *Liberty or Death: India's Journey to Independence and Division*. New York: HarperCollins, 1997.

Gandhi, Mohandas K. *An Autobiography: The Story of My Experiments with Truth*. Boston: Beacon Press, 1957.

Garrow, David J. *Bearing the Cross: Martin Luther King, Jr., and the Southern Christian Leadership Conference*. New York: William Morrow, 1986.

Gies, Frances. *Joan of Arc: The Legend and the Reality*. New York: Harper & Row, 1981.

Gilbert, Martin. *The Holocaust: A History of the Jews of Europe During the Second World War*. New York: Holt, Rinehart and Winston, 1985.

Girard, Philippe. *Toussaint Louverture: A Revolutionary Life*. New York: Basic Books, 2016.

Goodwin, Doris Kearns. *Team of Rivals: The Political Genius of Abraham Lincoln*. New York: Simon & Schuster, 2005.

Guha, Ramachandra. *Gandhi Before India*. New York: Knopf, 2014.

Henig, Ruth. *The League of Nations*. London: Haus Publishing, 2010.

Hilberg, Raul. *The Destruction of the European Jews*. New York: Holmes & Meier, 1985.

Hughes, Robert. *The Fatal Shore: The Epic of Australia's Founding*. New York: Knopf, 1987.

James, C. L. R. *The Black Jacobins: Toussaint L'Ouverture and the San Domingo Revolution*. New York: Dial Press, 1938.

Jordan, David P. *The King's Trial: Louis XVI vs. the French Revolution*. Berkeley: University of California Press, 1979.

Kapuscinski, Ryszard. *Shah of Shahs*. New York: Harcourt Brace Jovanovich, 1985.

Kranz, Gene. *Failure Is Not an Option: Mission Control from Mercury to Apollo 13 and Beyond*. New York: Simon & Schuster, 2000.

Lovell, Mary S. *The Sound of Wings: The Life of Amelia Earhart*. New York: St. Martin's Press, 1989.

MacCulloch, Diarmaid. *The Reformation: A History*. New York: Viking, 2003.

Macintyre, Stuart. *A Concise History of Australia*. Cambridge: Cambridge University Press, 1999.

Maier, Pauline. *Ratification: The People Debate the Constitution, 1787–1788*. New York: Simon & Schuster, 2010.

McCullough, David. *John Adams*. New York: Simon & Schuster, 2001.

McGirr, Lisa. *The War on Alcohol: Prohibition and the Rise of the American State*. New York: W. W. Norton, 2016.

McPherson, James M. *Battle Cry of Freedom: The Civil War Era*. New York: Oxford University Press, 1988.

Milani, Abbas. *The Shah*. New York: Palgrave Macmillan, 2011.

Murray, Charles, and Catherine Bly Cox. *Apollo: The Race to the Moon*. New York: Simon & Schuster, 1989.

Northedge, F. S. *The League of Nations: Its Life and Times, 1920–1946*. New York: Holmes & Meier, 1986.

Okrent, Daniel. *Last Call: The Rise and Fall of Prohibition*. New York: Scribner, 2010.

Paine, Thomas. *Common Sense*. Philadelphia: R. Bell, 1776.

Pernoud, Régine, and Marie-Véronique Clin. *Joan of Arc: Her Story*. New York: St. Martin's Press, 1998.

Pipes, Richard. *The Russian Revolution*. New York: Knopf, 1990.

Rich, Doris L. *Amelia Earhart: A Biography*. Washington, DC: Smithsonian Institution Press, 1989.

Richards, E. G. *Mapping Time: The Calendar and Its History*. Oxford: Oxford University Press, 1998.

Roper, Lyndal. *Martin Luther: Renegade and Prophet*. New York: Random House, 2017.

Schama, Simon. *Citizens: A Chronicle of the French Revolution*. New York: Knopf, 1989.

Seymour, Miranda. *Mary Shelley*. New York: Grove Press, 2000.

Shelley, Mary. *Frankenstein; or, The Modern Prometheus*. London: Lackington, Hughes, Harding, Mavor & Jones, 1818.

Shea, William R., and Mariano Artigas. *Galileo in Rome: The Rise and Fall of a Troublesome Genius*. Oxford: Oxford University Press, 2003.

Sobel, Dava. *Galileo's Daughter: A Historical Memoir of Science, Faith, and Love*. New York: Walker, 1999.

Somerset, Anne. *Elizabeth I*. New York: Knopf, 1991.

Starr, Kevin. *Golden Gate: The Life and Times of America's Greatest Bridge*. New York: Bloomsbury Press, 2010.

Tattersall, Robert. *Diabetes: The Biography*. Oxford: Oxford University Press, 2009.

Thomas, Nicholas. *Cook: The Extraordinary Voyages of Captain James Cook*. New York: Walker & Company, 2003.

Vaughan, Diane. *The Challenger Launch Decision: Risky Technology, Culture, and Deviance at NASA*. Chicago: University of Chicago Press, 1996.

Warner, Marina. *Joan of Arc: The Image of Female Heroism*. New York: Knopf, 1981.

Weir, Alison. *The Life of Elizabeth I*. New York: Ballantine Books, 1998.

Williams, Glyndwr, ed. *Captain Cook: Explorations and Reassessments*. Woodbridge: Boydell Press, 2004.

Wolpert, Stanley. *A New History of India*. Oxford: Oxford University Press, 1977.

Wood, Gordon S. *The Radicalism of the American Revolution*. New York: Knopf, 1992.

Image Credits

All images in this volume are sourced from public domain collections, government archives, and open-access institutional repositories. Images are used for educational, historical, and transformative commentary purposes.

Images were obtained from the following verified collections:

The Library of Congress, Prints and Photographs Division
U.S. National Archives and Records Administration
Smithsonian Institution Archives
National Aeronautics and Space Administration Image Library
British Library Digital Collections
Gallica, Bibliothèque nationale de France
The Metropolitan Museum of Art Open Access Collection
The Rijksmuseum Digital Collection
The National Portrait Gallery, London
The Vatican Library Digital Archive
This publication provides historical analysis, educational commentary, and contextual interpretation. Images are used to illustrate specific historical events, figures, and moments discussed in the accompanying text for purposes of criticism, comment, teaching, scholarship, and research.

ABOUT THE AUTHOR

Joel Thomas writes history as a record of pressure, consequence, and human error rather than triumphal myth. He is the creator of the Nomical History series, a calendar-based collection of daily and monthly volumes that examines how revolutions, collapses, discoveries, and disasters unfold when real people make decisions with limited information and imperfect judgment.

His work blends rigorous research with controlled irreverence, stripping away ceremonial storytelling to expose the machinery beneath historical events. Under the Nomical Books imprint, Thomas focuses on moments where systems break, authority fractures, and outcomes refuse to behave as intended.

He writes between archives, deadlines, and unfinished footnotes, driven by the belief that history becomes clearer, and more honest, when it is treated as something that happened rather than something that was meant to happen.

Learn more and connect at NomicalBooks.com or contact@nomicalbooks.com.